Praise for *Flawed Follower*

"Behind our performative masks and Sunday smiles, most of us feel inadequate, incompetent, and insecure about our discipleship to Jesus. But the life and failures of Peter offer us immense hope. As René reminds us, 'Jesus is never shocked, and welcomes us back, when we fall.' *Flawed Follower* is an inspiring, encouraging, and pragmatic guide for all those who find themselves struggling to measure up, exhausted trying to keep up, and on the brink of giving up."

- Jay Kim, Lead Pastor of WestGate Church, author of *Listen Listen Speak* and *Analog Christian*

"If you look closely in the mirror of Scripture, you can see yourself ... for better or for worse. In this piercingly honest book, Rene holds up the person of Peter and lets his story reflect on our own lives and souls. Read *Flawed Follower* with an open and humble heart and discover who you are and all God longs for you to be."

- Kevin G. Harney, Lead Pastor of Shoreline Church, Founder of Organic Outreach International, and author of *Organic Disciples*

"Peter has always held a special place in my heart. The disciple that Jesus most often publicly corrected ... imperfect, inconsistent, confused, *and* deeply loved and used by God. Rene takes the flawed person of Peter and centers him historically and creatively to make his story come alive in such rich ways. Don't miss using this extraordinary resource. I believe it will help churches more closely reflect the heart of God."

– Nancy Ortberg, CEO, Transforming the Bay with Christ, author of *Looking for God*

"Once again, René has created not just an insightful biblical study but one that is practical to every day living. Everyone can relate to the life of Peter in some way and it is super encouraging to read *Flawed Follower* to know that God loves us and has plans for us despite our failures and flaws."

- Dan Kimball, author of *How (Not) To Read the Bible*, Vice President of Western Seminary, founder of Vintage Faith Church

"René Schlaepfer combines marvelous writing, expositional skill, careful historical research, long pastoral insight into people and situations and narrative excellence into a profoundly moving account of his adventure of encounter with the biblical Peter and the Peter legacy. Read responsively and 'Follow Me' to eternal life in service to the gospel Peter lived and died for."

- Gerry Breshears, PhD, Professor of Theology, Western Seminary, Portland

"*Flawed Follower* is a brilliant, captivating look at the life and legacy of Peter. It is both encouraging and enlightening, a must read for anyone on their spiritual journey with Jesus. I highly recommend it!"

- Ken Foreman, Lead Pastor, Cathedral of Faith; Author, *Imagine Living Your Dreams*

HOPE FOR
IMPERFECT
INCONSISTENT
CONFUSED PEOPLE
WHO STILL LOVE JESUS

FLAWED FoLLOWER

TRAVELS WITH SIMON PETER

"FLAWED FOLLOWER: The Story of Simon Peter"
© 2024 René Schlaepfer

ISBNs: 978-1-7331971-5-1 (English pbk); 978-1-7331971-6-8 (English ebook); 8-1-7331971-7-5 (Spanish pbk); 978-1-7331971-8-2 (Spanish ebook)

Published by Twin Lakes Press, Aptos California
1st printing: 2024

Unless otherwise noted, scripture quotations are taken from THE HOLY BIBLE, NEW INTERNATIONAL VERSION®, NIV® Copyright © 1973, 1978, 1984, 2011 by Biblica, Inc.® Used by permission. All rights reserved worldwide.

Scripture quotations marked NLT are taken from the Holy Bible, New Living Translation, copyright © 1996, 2004, 2015 by Tyndale House Foundation. Used by permission of Tyndale House Publishers, Inc., Carol Stream, Illinois 60188. All rights reserved.

Scripture quotations marked (WEB) are taken from the WORLD ENGLISH BIBLE, public domain.

Scripture quotations marked (NET) are taken from the NET Bible® copyright ©1996-2006 by Biblical Studies Press, L.L.C. http://netbible.com All rights reserved. The names: THE NET BIBLE®, NEW ENGLISH TRANSLATION COPYRIGHT © 1996 BY BIBLICAL STUDIES PRESS, L.L.C. NET Bible® IS A REGISTERED TRADEMARK THE NET BIBLE® LOGO, SERVICE MARK COPYRIGHT © 1997 BY BIBLICAL STUDIES PRESS, L.L.C. ALL RIGHTS RESERVED

Scripture quotations marked ESV are from the ESV® Bible (The Holy Bible, English Standard Version®), copyright © 2001 by Crossway, a publishing ministry of Good News Publishers. Used by permission. All rights reserved.

Scripture quotations marked MSG are taken from THE MESSAGE, copyright © 1993, 2002, 2018 by Eugene H. Peterson. Used by permission of NavPress, represented by Tyndale House Publishers. All rights reserved.

Unless otherwise indicated, all photographs are by Jamie Rom or René Schlaepfer.

If you would like to reproduce or distribute any part of this publication, please contact: Twin Lakes Church, 2701 Cabrillo College Drive, Aptos, CA 95003-3103, USA or email info@tlc.org.

CONTENTS

PROLOGUE ix

1. WHEN JESUS CALLS 1

2. WHEN STORMS STRIKE 25

3. WHEN JESUS GETS CONFUSING 45

4. WHEN PANIC ATTACKS 65

5. WHEN THE PRESSURE GETS TO YOU 93

6. WHEN YOU HAVE FALLEN 115

7. WHEN SURPRISING DOORS OPEN 139

EPILOGUE 161

SMALL GROUP LESSONS 171

ENDNOTES 209

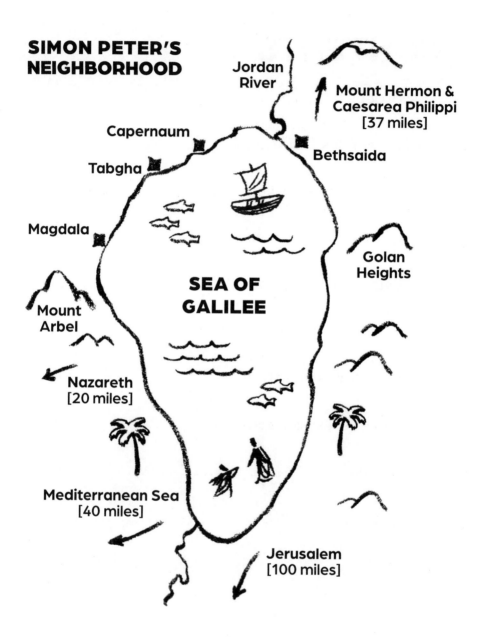

PROLOGUE

ROME
JULY 18, AD 64

The night is blazingly hot in the largest city on earth. Over a million people crowd together, restless, finding it hard to sleep. Somewhere a stray spark ignites nearby rags. Wind gusts quickly fan the flames into a blaze. Then, an inferno. When the fire is extinguished five days later, a third of the city lies in smoking ruin.

Roman citizens are stunned and furious. Rumors circulate that Emperor Nero deliberately started the blaze to clear the poorer neighborhoods for a lavish personal palace. Rebellion is brewing.

So Nero quickly finds a convenient scapegoat — the Christians.

Despite no evidence Christians are guilty, his soldiers drag thousands of these religious oddballs to a stadium known as Nero's Circus, a racetrack just outside the city walls near a place called Vatican Hill. Witnesses describe the emperor speeding giddily around his racetrack in a chariot as Christians die all around him, mauled by animals, crucified, and burned in a violent frenzy of retribution.

Nero's prize captive is Simon Peter, one of the leaders of the Christians, condemned to crucifixion in the center of the arena. But first, Peter makes an odd request: To be crucified upside-down. He feels unworthy to die in the same manner as his Lord. The Roman soldiers happily oblige.[1]

The violence-sated crowds slowly drift from the grandstands. Calm returns to the arena. Scavenging birds wheel in the sky. Then shadows flicker across the track: A few brave Christians hurriedly sneak in to claim Peter's body. They quickly lay it in a simple dirt grave across the street.

Roman Christians soon begin burying their dead around Peter's final resting place. A few decades later, they build a small memorial to Peter over the spot of his grave.[2] It is described in an ancient chronicle as "a niche flanked by two columns, covered with a coat of plaster painted red."[3] The shrine is about ten feet tall, nine feet wide, and less than two feet deep, attached to a red brick wall. For 150 years, believers visit the small shrine to pay their respects. Many scratch graffiti on the wall.

Then the monument suddenly disappears, hidden not by Roman enemies – but by the Christians themselves.

It will not be seen again for 1,700 years.

SEA OF GALILEE
PRESENT DAY

This is the story of how an untrained rural fisherman left his job, survived unthinkable disaster and personal failure and massive character flaws, and found himself leading a movement that outlasted the Roman Empire.

I have traveled 7,000 miles from my home in California to walk in the footsteps of Simon Peter, Jesus' first and most famous follower.

This is not a tourist trip. This is a pilgrimage. Because I need the transformation Peter experienced.

Peter could be impulsive and inconsistent. Inspired then inane. Committed but clueless. Daring and very dumb. Consequently, I relate to Peter more than any other character in the Bible!

Let me count the ways.

I heard someone say "Peter was one of those guys who walked into every room mouth first." Check. I call myself a "verbal processor," but there is usually lots of verbal and very little processing.

Peter was not showing any skill for spiritual leadership when Jesus called him. He's no monk. He's a swearing, sword-wielding sailor from a sketchy background. Again, check. I entered seminary with zero Christian education. My main job experience before becoming a pastor was as a Top 40 radio disc jockey. By day, I studied alongside serious students of the Bible who wondered if Christians should even drink beer, and by night, I worked with rock deejays who snorted cocaine and ate uppers like candy.

Peter defended Jesus, but often in very un-Christ-like ways. When Jesus is arrested, Simon Peter whips out his sword and attacks a guy, even though Jesus had been teaching him for three years to turn the other cheek. I, too, have defended my faith in ways more pushy than peaceful.

Peter could give in to peer pressure. I relate to that too. There are times I speak up when I should shut up and shut up when I should speak up.

Yet Peter's time with Jesus transformed this unqualified, unreliable, inconsistent, impetuous hothead into a courageous, consistent, and faithful leader.

How did that happen? I need to know. Because sometimes I still look more like Peter's "before" picture than his "after" picture.

I can praise Jesus with all my heart in church and then curse traffic with all my heart on the way home.

I can sincerely love people and then just as sincerely loathe people who disagree with me on some issue.

I can withstand serious temptation and then yield to stupid provocation.

That's why I'm drawn to Peter, who went from being as unstable as sand to being the Rock on which Jesus could build a movement.

Clearly Peter's transformation was not about his virtues. It was about Jesus, about his ability to take anyone and create an insightful, deeply spiritual influence for good.

So with Bible in hand, I am traveling in sequence from the very spot Peter first met Jesus to the place where he died—from Israel to Rome.

PROLOGUE

Along the way, I will fish where he fished, hike where he hiked, stand in the garden where he waved his sword, descend to the tomb he discovered empty, explore Roman ruins where he taught, and finally visit his long-lost final resting place.

I am seeking insight about how Jesus changes us. About what it means to follow Jesus even through questions and failures and betrayals. (Plus I thought it would be super fun!)

You can follow my journey through videos we filmed in all these places. You'll find them at **flawedfollower.com**. They also serve as discussion starters for the small group questions at the end of this book.

You may not relate to the same aspects of Peter's character that I do. You may not be an impulsive loudmouth (Thank God! There are enough of us already). Here's why Peter's story brings hope for you as well.

Peter is a very complex character. He has layers. He has contradictions. You and I are complex, too. We have mixed motives, lots of questions, quirky personalities. We can fear our complexity repulses Jesus, that he wants his disciples so focused we become one-dimensional weirdos.

Peter's story tells me Jesus can handle the complexity.

Maybe you've been thinking, "I'm drawn to Jesus, but I still have many questions about Jesus. I don't always understand Jesus. I don't always like Christians. Then there are my flaws. I find myself doing pretty well, and suddenly, I return to my old habits. I get jealous. I get petty. I get stupid. I can feel unworthy. Yet I am still attracted to Jesus. I can still be moved by Jesus. I want to serve Jesus. It's all inside me, all jumbled together."

In Peter, you'll find someone exactly like you.

Yes, Jesus transforms Peter into a world-changer. But that journey takes time, and Peter's moments of failure and confusion are part of how he gets there.

You may be wondering, exactly how did someone who misunderstood Jesus, contradicted Jesus, failed Jesus, denied Jesus, become the icon of what it means to follow Jesus?

That is what we are about to find out.

Let's go fishing.

1
WHEN JESUS CALLS
LUKE 5:1–11

ROME
AD 313

The Roman Emperor Constantine suddenly legalizes Christianity. Then he makes a (literally) monumental decision. He will build elaborate churches above spots long revered by Christians.

In Bethlehem, he builds a church over the cave thought to be the birthplace of Jesus.

In Jerusalem, he puts a shrine over the spot believed to have been Christ's tomb.

In Rome, he plans a massive structure over the humble memorial to Peter. The best engineers in the empire are called in. To create a level foundation, fill dirt from the hill is poured over the Roman cemetery that developed around Peter's small memorial. Peter's little shrine is encased in a giant marble box at the center of the building.

Over the centuries, Peter's grave is covered by more shrines and more marble, like giant Russian dolls, one monument over another. Later, Constantine's church is demolished, and an even more massive church is built in its place. Each time, Peter's actual grave is buried further and further underground until it is no longer accessible to visitors. Details about his modest tomb recede into myth. Some doubt it was ever there. Seventeen centuries go by.

Then a top-secret World War II archaeological expedition makes an astonishing discovery.

SEA OF GALILEE
PRESENT DAY

It's early morning, and I'm wearing three layers of clothes to fend off the chill as I board a boat ready to take me fishing on the Sea of Galilee. My captain today is Razi. His calloused hands and wind-creased face prove his lifelong passion for the lake; his family's been fishing here for generations.

"This boat," Razi exclaims proudly as he slaps it on its side, "is the oldest continuously operating vessel on the lake!" I don't want to say this out loud, but ... it shows. Let's just say the craft has character. It's been patched with fiberglass until its once graceful lines now bulge with signs of age (hey, I relate to that!).

The boat is small, just large enough for Razi's fishing equipment, his two-person crew, and me. I anticipate a great catch of the tilapia crowding these waters. Thirteen miles from north to south, eight miles at its widest, the Sea of Galilee is the lowest freshwater lake in the world. It's full of fish, so it's easy to find people here who love fishing. Like Razi.

Or like Hod, a young, dreadlocked marine archaeologist.

Or Yaron, an amateur diver who fishes here with his bare hands.

Razi, Hod, Yaron. You'll meet them all again later as we follow in the wake of the most famous of all Galilee fishermen.

Simon Peter.

FLAWED FOLLOWER

He is a famed fisherman, even though, when you think about it, he never seemed to be very good at it. We never see him catch a thing unless Jesus does a miracle.

He became a famous follower of Jesus, too, though he often failed at that as well: Peter denied Jesus, disagreed with Jesus, argued with Jesus, and most of the time just didn't get Jesus.

I love this guy.

I love him precisely because he is so flawed. That's encouraging to me because I find my own shortcomings to be so spectacular that they cause me to marvel.

Let me share a few.

One of the most basic skills for a pastor is to actually know the names of people in your church — a skill I can't seem to master after decades of trying. I once forgot the name of a woman in our congregation even after she had told me three times. Her name was René.

I'm astonishingly unmechanical. After my hopeful handyman father-in-law gave me an electric drill for Christmas, I tried to put up our new mini-blinds by myself. After all, they were called something like Five-Minute E-Z Blinds for Morons. Their logo was a cartoon monkey with a screwdriver. After an hour of increasingly maddening attempts, the screws kept popping out toward me as if they were possessed. My wife walked up, watched for a minute while sipping her coffee, and then gently broke it to me that I had been using the drill in reverse the entire time. Outdone by a cartoon monkey.

I'm so unathletic that I strike out in whiffle ball. I get so tongue-tied that once I accidentally swore during a sermon when I tried to say, "the ship fits." I'm an anxious, forgetful, clumsy doofus.

And my inadequacies go deeper, down into my character. On my good days, I am patient, kind, wise. On my bad days, I am petty, angry, sarcastic, and weak when tempted.

It adds up.
I can feel like:
A bad friend.
A hypocrite as a leader.
A failure as a Jesus follower.
I don't deserve to have this mantle of leadership.
I may as well quit and hand it to a cartoon monkey.

I have a feeling I'm not alone. Do these thoughts ever haunt you? "I'm unqualified. I'm overwhelmed. I'm inconsistent. I'm just too flawed."

Then Simon Peter's story is for you too. He felt exactly the same way.

Peter is the relatable disciple. The very first generation of Christians thought so. They loved his story. Peter is mentioned in the gospels over 120 times. To put this in perspective: The disciple John is mentioned about twenty times, as is Judas. Andrew is mentioned twelve times. Thomas is mentioned ten times. Peter is mentioned more than anyone else but Jesus. In fact, in nearly every recorded episode in the life of Christ, Peter is somewhere close. Peter's eyes are the main windows through which we see Jesus.

But Peter's portrayal is far from flattering. Peter has an ego. Peter gets cocky. Peter is comically blind to his weaknesses.

How did a guy like that gain any credibility as a leader? Oh, and how do we even *know* these stories about Peter?

I want to share a discovery about that last question that astonished me. Mark (as in, the guy who wrote the Gospel of Mark) was Simon Peter's assistant and traveled with him. The earliest Christian leaders were unanimous that Mark wrote his gospel based on Peter's own stories. Then Matthew and Luke used Mark as a source for their own gospels.[4] That means these stories of Peter's flaws and failures... *came from Peter.*

Why would Peter tell these unflattering stories about himself?

Peter had something to say to all those intrigued by Jesus, then and now: **Start the journey.** No matter how unqualified you think you are. **Stay on the journey.** No matter how often you fail.

Razi anchors his boat in the shallows near offshore springs that have attracted fish since Peter's day. He's hopeful we'll catch some lunch.

"You are in the right spot now, you have the right crew, and you are in the right boat – the oldest continuously operating fishing boat on the lake," he announces again as he slaps the bow. A small piece of fiberglass plops into the water for emphasis. "Now we wait!"

We drop the net into the water. And sit. And stare.

The sunrise casts ripples of gold onto the lake. Blue-veined dragonflies skim the surface. A white egret is fishing in the reeds.

Then Razi feels it's time. We haul in the net ... and one solitary sardine wriggles in the mesh. He is not even afraid. He is just mocking us. We throw him back to his more elusive brethren. As we putter dejectedly back toward the harbor, a gull hovers over us, hunting for a snack. When he works out that we don't have a single fish for him to steal, he tells us off with seagull swearwords and flaps away in disgust.

I watch and imagine how a similar bird must have encountered the same frustration one morning nearly 2,000 years ago.

SEA OF GALILEE
AD 30

Fishing boats slide wearily back into their wharves at Capernaum, their occupants tired, aching, and hungry after a night of net fishing on the dark water. Gulls glide, hoping for scraps.

We see the most courageous bird now swooping closer, attempting theft. But our daring gull is grumpy today because the boats have few fish. He screams and soars into the sunrise.

If he had been capable of reflection, his mood might have improved with the thought that, despite today's meager pickings, the first century is a great time to be a seagull in Galilee.

Stretching below him are 14 harbors with breakwaters, piers, and wharves constructed by the Roman-allied state. The fishing industry is booming because the Roman overlords cannot get enough of their beloved "fish sauce," the ketchup of antiquity, used to flavor every dish (and even many drinks!).

What doesn't go into fish sauce is pickled or dried for local lunches – think fish jerky.

Seven thermal springs bubble up near the beaches here and overflow into the lake, creating pockets of warm water. Warm water means more algae. More algae means more fish. More fish mean more fish sauce.

The Galilee region will never be more prosperous. New construction in the Roman style ripples across the hills around the shore: palaces, warehouses, homes, theaters.

And roads. Especially roads.

Roads to transport troops.

Roads to welcome merchants.

Roads to move fish sauce.

The longest of the roads, the beautifully paved Via Maris, edges Capernaum, connecting the modest fishing village with the entire world.

Our gull doesn't care. His gut still growling, he considers a breakfast of rotting fruit. Vineyards roll down every hill. Fig and olive orchards carpet each valley. But it's spring, and the fruit is still green.

So the sulky seabird glides east to inspect boats docking at Bethsaida, a small fishing port just three miles away, but their decks are as bereft of fish as the rest. Our bird turns and eyes his usual emergency option.

Just a few miles from Capernaum is the site of a major fish-processing installation called Magdala. Two massive wharves, one the length of a football field and another 230 feet long, jut into the lake. A glass factory and pottery shop craft jars for the end product. The whole city is a well-oiled fish sauce machine.

If only our bird had the power to ponder what he is seeing, he would know that the entire landscape of Simon Peter's early life stretches beneath him: Capernaum, where Simon lived. Bethsaida, where he was born. Magdala, where he marketed his fish.

Instead our gull eyes Magdala's 40 large fish tanks and decides to risk diving for a treat. As he glides in for his heist, on the ground below him the day is already growing warmer, and families are growing hungry for breakfast.

Sailors secure boats.

Fishermen mend nets.

Bakers deliver bread.

And a small crowd gathers around a newcomer.

A man fishing. But not for fish.

This is Day One of the Jesus Movement, the moment Jesus calls his first disciples.

Jesus stands at the shoreline teaching. People crowd toward him, listening, jostling, pushing, and soon he's ankle-deep in water. He looks around and sees two empty fishing boats left on shore by the crew now washing out their nets. Their defeated body language makes it clear they haven't caught a thing all night.

His next move tells us a lot about Jesus. He could have chosen his first followers from the educated, religious elite. Instead, he deliberately seeks out the least likely, least qualified, least educated to be his closest apprentices.

Fishermen.

Romans loved fish but complained endlessly about fishermen. One ancient writer, Athenaeus, collected quotes mocking the fish industry from pundits of the day. His list of putdowns runs for pages, featuring gems like:

> "... when I see the fishmongers, of all tribes far the worst, bending their sulky eyes down to the ground ... I am disgusted ...

> "I used to think the race of fishmongers was only insolent in Attica; but now I see that like wild beasts they are savage by nature, everywhere the same."

Other choice words used in his text to describe them: moody, stubborn, and homicidal.[5]

Jesus sees them and thinks: Perfect!

He climbs into Simon's boat and asks him to set out just a little way from shore to give him a buffer from the crowd.

Simon. Trendy name at the time. There are at least nine Simons in the New Testament. One of Jesus' brothers was named Simon. Two of the twelve disciples were named Simon.

Why so popular? Because people hoped for another revolution.

One hundred sixty-four years before Simon Peter was born, the famed Jewish revolutionary Simon the Maccabee and his brothers John, Judas, Jonathan, Eleazar and their father Mattathias kicked out the oppressive Syrian Greek rulers and liberated the Jews in a great war of independence. It's still remembered every year at Hannukah. Half the original disciples were named after members of this heroic Maccabee family (Simon twice, Judas twice, John, and Matthew). That tells us patriotic Jewish parents were instilling stories of revolution in their kids' heads.[6]

Their imaginations were primed. They were just waiting for another hero.

Simon pushes the boat gently from shore. Jesus sits down and teaches. Ribbons of light reflect off the water and play on his face. Simon watches. And listens.

When Jesus is finished, the sun's high. He turns to Simon and, in what I take as payment for use of his boat, tells him,

> "Put out into deep water, and let down the nets for a catch." (Luke 5:4)

Simon must have thought, "Oh-kay, here's a landlubber."

Two things wrong with Jesus' suggestion: First, net fishing in Galilee is done best near the shore, not out in deep water. Second, it's best at night, not in broad daylight.

If you're fishing with a lure, you go out during the day so fish can see the bait. If you're fishing with a net, you go out in the dark, making the net less visible. In those days, crews lit oil lamps at night to attract fish. I see the same strategy in my hometown during squid season. Boats go out at night and lure squid into nets with massive lights.

> Simon answered, "Master, we've worked hard all night and haven't caught anything. But because you say so, I will let down the nets." (Luke 5:5)

"If *you* say so," said Peter, dubiously.
Out they row.
Down goes the net.
Instantly, schools of fish catapult themselves into the trap.

Simon yells at his crew to get in the other boat and help. The massive catch pulls both boats so far over they nearly sink before they wobble back to shore, where Simon falls at Jesus' feet and exclaims,

"Go away from me, Lord; I am a sinful man!" (Luke 5:8b)

When Simon says, "Lord," it's a title of respect, but not yet worship. Simon's unsure who Jesus is. But he knows who *he* is. A sinner. And this miracle worker freaks him out. *Move on, Master. This is not for me. I'm not good enough.*

Ever wonder if you're good enough for God?

I've heard the excuse a hundred times when people find out I'm a pastor: "The ceiling of the church would fall in if I ever visited!" Listen. *None* of us measures up to God's perfect standards. We *all* sin and fall short of his glory.

But what if God is not primarily interested in performance?

What if God is interested in something else, like a relationship?

What if you didn't *have* to be good enough for God?

What if God took care of that for you?

What if God called sinners to himself rather than perfect people? Wouldn't that be awesome?

Well, that's what this is all about. Jesus calls the least likely suspects.

And not just Simon Peter. Think of the other disciples in this scene.

Andrew? This is the guy who will later say to Jesus, "There is a boy here who has five loaves and two fish, but what good are these among so many?" Mister Eeyore.

Or James and John. These are the sages always asking Jesus things like, "Will you do for us whatever we want? Can we be the most important people in heaven? Can we call down fire to consume unbelievers?" (Jesus says no, no, and no.)

Jesus is about to invite Thomas, who, when later told Jesus is resurrected, says not just, "I do not believe it," but "I *will* not believe it!"

Jesus invited Simon the Zealot. Many Zealots were armed insurrectionists. He will deliver Mary of Magdala from her demons.

Jesus is clearly not hiring based on resumés.

Notice that Jesus does not contradict Peter when he says he is a sinful man. What Jesus says is,

"Don't be afraid." (Luke 5:10b)

So often, what keeps us from following Jesus is fear.
Fear of what my cool friends will say.
Fear of what I might have to change.
Fear of leaving my routine.
Fear of looking stupid.
Fear I'll fail again.
And all of that might happen. It did for Peter.
But Jesus gives him a purpose.

"Come, follow me," Jesus said. (Matthew 4:19a)

Follow me.
Locked into those two simple words is what it means to be a Christian.
First word: **Follow.**

Not, "Understand me perfectly."

Not, "Pass this theology test."

Not, "Sign this statement of faith and conduct."

Not even, "Before we begin, let me clarify a few things."

Just, "Follow." Hang out. Watch and listen and learn and serve.

Peter and his friends had no clue what was ahead. They were extremely fuzzy about who Jesus was, and Jesus didn't go out of his way to explain much, either.

Too often, we can make it seem like following Jesus is about passing a theology exam. But the invitation is not to comprehend Jesus. It's to *follow* Jesus. Tag along. Learn more. And allow yourself to be changed in the *process*.

Second word: **Me**.

It's all about *Jesus*.

My kids had excellent questions about their faith as they grew. What about all those strange Old Testament laws handed down by Moses? What about those brutal battles waged by Joshua? What about the Crusades? What about modern American politicians or pastors who claim to be Christians and act reprehensibly?

Great questions, with an intriguing variety of possible answers. But the big picture, as we discussed together, is that we are not Moses-ians, Joshua-ians, Crusade-ians, or American-Christian-culture-ians. We are *Christ*ians.

We are about following *Christ*.

"...and I will send you out to fish for people."
(Matthew 4:19b)

When Apple computer co-founder Steve Jobs recruited Pepsi's John Sculley to be Apple's CEO, he famously asked him, "Do you want to sell sugar water for the rest of your life, or do you want to change the world?" Sculley moved to Apple.[7]

Jesus is asking Peter, "Do you want to sell fish sauce for the rest of your life, or do you want to change the world?"

> At once they left their nets and followed him.
> (Matthew 4:20)

Peter and his friends were not yet committed Christians. But they were intrigued. This story is not really about their decision; it's pointing us to Jesus and telling us something about how he operates. He comes to you and me in the middle of our busy lives and says, simply, "Follow me." **It's not about your worthiness, your performance, your potential. It's about his generous grace.**

Because what Jesus did in calling these grown adults was radical. Here's how teachers usually found disciples in those days. If you were thought to be exceptionally bright at age 15, rabbis interviewed you. If accepted, you studied with them until you were thirty and became a rabbi. This was very prestigious. It's what every parent wanted for their son. If you were not chosen, you entered a trade by age 18. Even within the trades, there was hierarchy—the most prestigious involved artistic skill or precision, like stone masonry or mosaic design. Among the least prestigious was fishing. No wonder they were sulky. They hadn't made the cut. Not good enough to get picked.

Maybe you can identify. You sometimes get that feeling you used to have when teams got picked in school: All the teams around you are picked. But no one has picked you.

Perhaps a spouse, a boss, a ministry leader, a school, a boyfriend, a girlfriend has even said, "I do not pick you anymore."

Today, Jesus calls *you*.
Brennan Manning wrote,

"...Grace calls out, 'You are not just a disillusioned old man who may die soon, a middle-aged woman stuck in a job and desperately wanting to get out, a young person feeling the fire in the belly begin to grow cold. You may be insecure, inadequate, mistaken or potbellied. Death, panic, depression, and disillusionment may be near you. But you are not just that. You are accepted.' Never confuse your perception of yourself with the mystery that you really are accepted."[8]

Jesus says, I pick you. I choose you. You'll be a fisher of people. You'll be part of the kingdom of heaven blossoming into earth.

Harvard Professor Arthur C. Brooks details what research has discovered about the formation of religious faith – or any lifelong commitment.[9]

There are three components: practice, feelings, and beliefs. In that order.

First, you start the **practice**. You attend church, read the Bible, pray, do a Bible study (like this!), join a small group, experience worship.

Second, **feelings** begin to bubble. You are moved by a verse, calmed by prayer, enjoy fellowship.

Third, you are motivated to study the **beliefs**. You start investigating intellectually. You are moved to faith.

Practices, feelings, beliefs. When you think about it, that's the order in which you discover anything in life.

It's how you learn a sport. You **try** it; you **enjoy** it; and then you **learn** more about it.

It's how you find a spouse. You **date**; you continue if you **feel** attraction; you make **decisions** about your partner.

This is the *reverse* of what we often assume to be the path to faith. We imagine an intellectual decision about conversion first. Then, the feelings come. Then if I am really mature, I finally develop the practices.

But that's not the order in which Jesus develops the disciples, is it? First, they know almost nothing about him. They tag along. They listen. Observe. Help. Finally, they draw conclusions based on what they have seen and learned.

So if you've been thinking about this Jesus stuff, why not try it the Jesus way? You can move in the direction of Jesus even if you don't understand Jesus or fully believe in Jesus. That's what the disciples did.

Bryce Edwards would agree. He's a young staff member at the church where I'm a pastor. Coming out of high school, Bryce had no sense of direction in life. "I didn't know what I wanted to do and I kept chasing things that always left me empty," he told me. "I had never heard the gospel at that point, and didn't even know that having a relationship with Jesus was possible."

Then some friends invited him to our church college group. After saying no a handful of times, he finally accepted their invitation.

"Even though I didn't care for the message, I felt a strong sense of belonging. Over the next year, I kept going for the community aspect, and little by little, I started paying more attention to the gospel. After a year of wrestling with the idea of God, I put my faith in him!" Fast-forward one year: Bryce began working at the very place where he found his faith. He says, "God reached me and is now using me to help others grow closer to Him."

He began following. He became a fisher of people. Sounds like Peter.

Bryce is not alone. Elizabeth Oldfield calls herself "a failed atheist." While working for the BBC in London, she found herself dissatisfied with the bleakness of modern secular life. She longed for the community and clarity of Christianity. Yet she just didn't believe. After some warm and intelligent friends invited her to their church, she began to attend with them and found a way of living and loving that eventually drew her into faith. Her invitation to atheists and doubters is this: try the Christian path, even if you aren't sure about its truth claims. As she puts it, "Lay down the burden of knowing exactly what you *believe* and take up some life-giving *behaviors*."[10]

In other words, follow first. Tag along. Hang out. God may surprise you with faith.

OK, but if you've already decided to follow Jesus, then what sustains you? I want to reiterate three points I made in my book *Jesus Journey*:

1. Stay astonished that Jesus calls you.

> "You did not choose me, but I chose you and appointed you that you should go and bear fruit ..." (John 15:16)

Jesus picked average people doing ordinary things. They weren't showing promise. He wasn't picking proven A-players. He was showing what he can do with *anyone*.

God can do more with a nobody than anybody else can do with a somebody! That's a fact proven again and again in the gospels. Jesus just needs a willing spirit, a mustard seed, a few biscuits and fish, some mud and spit, and a miracle happens.

Another Brennan Manning quote:

> "We should be astonished at the goodness of God, stunned that he should bother to call us by name, our mouths wide open at his love, bewildered that at this very moment we are standing on holy ground."[11]

Don't keep putting yourself down. That voice in your head is not Jesus. He knows how flawed you are. Yet he keeps calling you.

2. See others as Jesus sees you.
Even though Jesus graced the disciples, they could find it hard to grace others. As Jesus told them one day when they were surrounded by Samaritans they saw as enemies:

> "Wake up and look around. The fields are ripe for harvest."
> (John 4:35)

See others like Jesus saw you when he called you. See them with the eyes of grace. No matter how unlikely they may seem.

3. Stay focused on Jesus.
This is not just how to *start* your journey with Jesus; it's how to *continue* your journey with Jesus. Don't get distracted. Controversies, debates, and issues du jour will lure you. "Follow me" was our first invitation, and "follow me" remains the key.

It's that simple. Those two words. "Follow me."

During that long wait for our lone sardine, Razi and I drift into conversation. I ask, "Have you ever encountered a fierce, sudden storm on this lake, like the ones the Bible talks about?"

"Well, you know," he says, "This (slap!) is the oldest continuously operating fishing boat on the Sea of Galilee, so yes, it has seen storms. Many, many storms." Then his hoarse voice drops to a whisper. "But one time, I even cry and cry and cry. That time, I think ... I will die."

Simon Peter is about to feel that same cold dread.

Watch a short video for this chapter filmed on location

DIGGING DEEPER
PETER'S FISH

Ever wonder what kind of fish Peter and Jesus ate? In his fascinating book *The Sea of Galilee and Its Fishermen in the New Testament*, long-time Galilee fisherman Mendel Nun explains that 18 species of indigenous fish live in the lake.[*] The most popular for dining: musht, or tilapia, including *Tilapia Galilea*, commonly called Saint Peter's Fish; carp; and sardines. Lots of sardines. Tons are still caught here every night at the height of the fishing season. Sardines were the most commercial fish in the New Testament era too, made into "fish sauce" or preserved through drying and pickling.

The gospels describe Simon Peter and his partners working two ships, which probably indicates a "purse seine" method, with a long net strung between boats and slowly gathered up between them. Archaeologists have discovered 14 commercial harbors here from Peter's time, many quite sophisticated, some with wharves as long as football fields.

Or you could fish like my friend and Israeli tour guide Yaron. He grew up in Tiberias and often fishes for tilapia here. Not with a line and lure. Not with a net. But by hand! Yaron waits until the sun goes down, grabs a flashlight, pops on his swim goggles and fins, and hops in. In the winter, fish gather even closer to shore, where the hot springs flow. As Yaron says, "It's like a jacuzzi for fish!" He swims up slowly, blinds the fish with his flashlight, grabs them, stuffs them in his swim shirt, and... home for dinner!

[*] Mendel Nun, *The Sea of Galilee and Its Fishermen in the New Testament*, (Tiberias: Kinnereth Sailing Co, 1989)

2
WHEN STORMS STRIKE
MATTHEW 14:22–33

ROME
1940

It is getting crowded in the crypt.

The astonishing 440-foot dome designed by Michelangelo soars high over the altar of St. Peter's Basilica. The vast sanctuary, covered with gold, silver, and marble, can hold 22,000 people.

But below the sanctuary is a dimly lit burial chamber known as the Sacred Grottoes—the church's basement. Coffins of emperors, kings, queens, and popes line the walls, dead deal-makers and power-brokers from 17 centuries of European history.

Pope Pius XI wants to be buried here. But space is running out. So, in February 1939, a decision is made to enlarge the cramped crypt into a nice chapel.

But you know how it goes with remodels. You start one thing, and then you find another...

The pope feels the ceilings are too low—they're only about 8 feet high—but they can't be raised since this is the basement. Solution: Lower the floor. Ancient marble slabs are pried up. Workers begin excavating the packed dirt below.

But almost immediately, they are surprised by the dead.

First, colorful paintings of flowers, dolphins, and the goddess Venus are revealed. Then something grislier. A skeleton—the partially decayed remains of a woman. Around her skull are traces of golden hair netting. A thick gold bracelet still encircles her left wrist. The diggers soon realize this is a tomb; its roof had been removed ages before and quickly filled in with soil. Then they find another similar grave. Then another.

Soon a complete underground neighborhood emerges, with streets and alleyways, but instead of homes, there are tombs. What is this place?

Archaeologists are called in, and on their recommendation, the pope allows a full-scale excavation. But he insists on one crucial rule: Their exploration is to remain top-secret. They cannot even use power tools for fear they might be heard in the church above. Digging is to be done by hand, as quietly as possible.[12]

After all, the workers have found something the faithful might find scandalous.

The holiest church in Christendom is built over pagan graves.

SEA OF GALILEE, ISRAEL
PRESENT DAY

I glide across the surface of the sea. Standing on the water, I peer down into the lake's depths. Warm waves caress my bare feet. White tilapia swim just beneath me. A fiberglass chunk of Razi's boat floats by.

The morning scene is mesmerizing. Suddenly, I slide into turbulence, rocking up and down. I look up. The wind is intensifying. White-capped breakers stream toward me.

Good thing I'm on a paddleboard.

My guide, Hod Froilch, and I plunge our paddles into the water and maneuver into a lagoon where the lake is calmer. We sit on our boards, and Hod breaks out his special blend of herbal tea and some fresh fruit. Time for breakfast!

I'm staying at the Nof Ginosar kibbutz on the Galilee shore, where I've met Hod, a young marine archaeology student. Born and raised here, Hod is a third-generation Galilee fisherman. As a side hustle, he and his wife Charlotte started "Mister Ananas Surf," a windsurf and SUP rental shack. "Ananas" means pineapple (yes, they are grown in Israel), and his company's goofy mascot is a sunglasses-wearing pineapple that totally suits Hod's personality. He's a laid-back, dread-locked, always-smiling twenty-something who would fit perfectly on Maui.

Back home, I'm a passionate ocean paddleboarder, and one of my dreams has been to do some stand-up on the Sea of Galilee. So Hod met me on the rocky shoreline when it was still dark, and we set out. The sun rose halfway through our adventure, reflecting off glassy water. I squinted so I couldn't see my board and imagined I was walking on water. Like Jesus. Like Peter too. Sort of.

I've lived in Santa Cruz, California, for decades. Water means fun there. Santa Cruz is even in the lyrics of a Beach Boys song ("Surfing USA," if you're interested—and you should be). It's the quintessential California beach town. People there love surfing, sailing, swimming, stand-up paddle boarding. You see the same sports in Israel. *Today*. But in Jesus' time, the sea was seen as sinister.

In Hebrew Scripture, whether you meant the ocean or large lakes like the Sea of Galilee, the sea was ominous, not frivolous. It seems to represent the Israelites' deepest, most ancient fears. Almost every time the sea is mentioned, it's a place of unpredictable floods, storms, and waves—chaos so powerful only God's power can vanquish it. Psalm 65:7 speaks of Yahweh, the Lord, as the only one able to "... still the roaring of the seas, the roaring of their waves."

The Sea of Galilee is still a hazardous body of water. As recently as 1992, 10-foot-high waves crashed into downtown Tiberias, flooding the city and destroying millions of dollars of property. My fishing friend Razi told me that storms here can be so intense that they test the nerves of the most experienced captain. He recalled, "One time, I cry and cry. I think, for sure, I will die." During the tempest, Razi hung on to his swamped boat, thinking it would sink at any moment. After the storm passed, he was too tired to row back or even start his engine. He just laid in the bottom of the boat, shaking with exhaustion, until his brother rescued him.

I've experienced it, too, to a lesser degree. One day, I was sailing on the Sea of Galilee when sunny blue skies were replaced by dark clouds and frigid, pelting rain within minutes. Because of the heat earlier in the day, we were all in flip-flops and shorts. Midway through the one-hour cruise, we needed raincoats and boots. One minute we could see the shore. The next minute, we had no idea where we were.

Here's why this happens. The lake sits in a narrow weather tunnel, the deep Jordan Rift Valley. It's the longest and lowest earthquake fault on the earth's surface. Cold air blows down from the often snow-covered Mount Hermon range, just 20 miles north but 10,000 feet higher. From the south, super-heated air comes up from the Dead Sea region, at 1,400 feet below sea level, the lowest desert on the planet. When cold air and hot air collide over water, things get interesting.

Jesus has just fed five thousand people through the miracle of the loaves and fishes. He needs some quiet time. He heads to a nearby mountain for prayer and tells the disciples to go ahead of him in their boat to their next destination.

> Later that night, he was there alone, and the boat was already a considerable distance from land, buffeted by the waves because the wind was against it. Shortly before dawn Jesus went out to them, walking on the lake. (Matthew 14:23b-25)

During my stay at Nof Ginosar, I slid across the same lake. With a board. On glassy waters. Yet Jesus glides through rollers on foot, like an elegant, unruffled ice skater.

> When the disciples saw him walking on the lake, they were terrified. "It's a ghost," they said, and cried out in fear. (Matthew 14:26)

The disciples are showing how influenced they were by Roman and Greek culture because there was no theology of ghosts in the Jewish religion.[13] But all the modern Hollywood horror-movie tropes about spirits and haunted houses are found in pagan Roman writings from the first century.

The Roman writer Pliny the Younger told a ghost story about a house haunted by a chain-rattling spirit. The owners later discovered the corpse of a murdered man buried in the yard, entwined with chains. They exhumed and reburied the body with proper rituals, and the ghost never reappeared. These sorts of stories were *hugely* popular in the ancient world and clearly influenced the imaginations of the disciples.

This is an example of a phenomenon I see today as a pastor: Devout Christians getting freaked out by superstitions about the spirit world that owe far more to paganism than to Scripture. The disciples were in a stressful situation, but their unfounded fears just made it worse. **We must let our imaginations be crafted by the gospel, not guesses, gossip, or ghost stories.** Because in the storms, our imaginations run wild.

> But Jesus immediately said to them: "Take courage! It is I. Don't be afraid." (Matthew 14:27)

In the original Greek, Jesus says just five words.

Tharseite! Ego eimi. Me phobeisthe.

The phrase reads like this in English: "Courage! I am! No fear."[14]

I love the power-packed brevity of it.

Look at it more closely.

First: *Courage.*

The Greek word *tharseite* is variously translated into English as "be comforted," "take courage," "take heart." The root word means "to radiate warm confidence."

Into the cold storm come warm words.

Then: *It is I.*

The original two-word Greek is punchier: *ego eimi.* I am.

Jesus loved those two words. He uses them seven times in the Gospel of John to start sentences that describe his identity:

I am the bread of life.

I am the light of the world.

I am the door.

I am the good shepherd.

I am the resurrection and the life.

I am the way, the truth, and the life.

I am the true vine.

Here in Matthew, he stops after the first two.

I am. Period.

To fully understand what he's saying (and how it's a clue to his identity), you have to go back to Moses, about 1,400 years before Christ. When Moses asked God his name, the Lord responded,

> "I am who I am. This is what you are to say to the Israelites: 'I am has sent me to you.'" (Exodus 3:14)

What is God's name? *I am.*

When Jesus uses those words, he is giving his disciples more than just reassurance that he's *not* a ghost. He's giving them a hint about who he *is.*

Finally: *Don't be afraid.*

This is God's most frequently spoken sentence to humans in the Bible. He says it more than 140 times. From God's perspective, we really, really need to hear this.

Now put it all together.

Courage. I am. Don't be afraid.

Where in your life is Jesus saying that to you right now?

That pending physical exam. The school test. The job change. The cancer. The long road of grief. The struggle with recovery. The nagging buzz of chronic anxiety. Worries about your kids, your country, your church.

Courage. I am. Don't be afraid.

So here it comes—the big moment. Jesus is about to calm those waves. What a great ending to the story! I picture Jesus approaching the boat, hands lifted to the storm, clearing his throat, the disciples starting to calm down as they anticipate the miracle.

All interrupted. By Peter. Of course.

Um, uh, uh, excuse me. Just a second. I have a special request. I see the other guys looking at him, "Seriously? Now?!"

"Lord, if it's you," Peter replied, "tell me to come to you on the water." (Matthew 14:28)

What is Peter thinking? I do not have the slightest idea. Why not, "Lord, if it's you, calm the storm?" As so often with Peter, he seems out of sync socially. Peter's the clueless guy at the wedding who, when everyone's focused on the best man's toast, is trying to start a game of charades.

Other disciples: "Hurray! We're saved!"

Peter: "Hey! Can I try that?"

Jesus says, oh, all right, come on. Peter gets out of the boat. He starts doing it—walking on the water toward Jesus!

> But when he saw the wind, he was afraid and, beginning to sink, cried out, "Lord, save me!" (Matthew 14:30)

Enthusiasm fizzles into fear. He starts to sink—when his focus shifts from the *Savior* to the *storm*.

Easy to do.

The storms of life are intense, distracting, loud.

Waves splashing, wind howling.

The cultural storms, political storms, health storms, financial storms, relational storms.

The storms can seem more real than Jesus. They are louder. They are more visible.

But the Savior is stronger than the storms you can see.

> Immediately Jesus reached out his hand and caught him. "You of little faith," he said, "why did you doubt?"
> (Matthew 14:31)

Three principles here for navigating your own storms.

1. Request guidance.

This story has been seen for centuries as a great example of the risk-taking faith we should all dare to have. I'm a preacher, so I'll admit I love to use this story as an illustration of *action*. "Do you have faith? Then get out of the boat!" It's a great one for a building campaign, a mission trip, or a volunteer drive.

But are we guilty of adapting this to our initiative-taking, "Go West, young man!" American mentality when we emphasize that part of the story? We risk focusing on ourselves and our bravado instead of Jesus.

Not every leap is a leap of faith. After all, Satan asked Jesus to take a leap, too—a leap right off the top of the temple. The devil even quoted Scripture. Very motivational! Yet Jesus flatly refused. Certainly not because he lacked faith. But because *that* leap wasn't God's will.

I've seen people use this story as an excuse for all kinds of hare-brained ideas. They leap forward, then wonder why God didn't bless their move. Note: Even Peter doesn't just plop into the water. He asks Jesus first and waits for his answer.

God-honoring leaps of faith need to consider what Christians call "the whole counsel of God," the big picture of the Bible, plus any specific instruction for your situation in God's word and wise counsel from wise people.

However, if some Christians err by justifying anything as a leap of faith that Jesus is obligated to honor, others err by not trying anything. They miss the second part of Peter's example: When it's Christ calling, Peter goes for it.

2. Respond to guidance.

When you know God's will, act. Immediately. Peter gets out of the boat. You can rightly criticize Peter for his impulsiveness at times, but know this: Action does breed courage. Procrastination produces anxiety. When you know what you should be doing, *not* doing it only makes you more afraid of it.

As John Ortberg memorably puts it, don't be a "boat potato."[15]

Obedience delayed is opportunity missed. Maybe you know exactly what God wants you to do but you're afraid to try. One point of this story is that **you can do whatever Jesus asks you to do, no matter what.**

I'll tell you some ways Jesus is directing you, based on Scripture. He's inviting you to forgive an enemy. To stop worrying. To serve him by feeding the hungry, by visiting the sick, by teaching the young. To stay holy in an impure world. To stop that destructive habit. And it all seems impossible to you. Like, walking-on-water-level impossible.

But it's *Jesus* asking you, so you can do it. Get out of that boat.

3. Refocus on the guide.

When I learned to stand-up paddleboard on the Pacific Ocean (not a lake with flat water, but Monterey Bay, where waves can reach world-class heights), my veteran surfer friends told me, "Keep your eyes on the horizon. Do not look down at your feet or the waves."

Once I followed their advice, it kept me upright in some pretty intense (or as they would say, gnarly) situations. It works almost like a miracle. *Eyes up.*

But it's challenging instruction to follow! When waves are washing over your board, you feel cold water swirl around your feet, you're lifted up and down on the surge, everything inside of you compels you to look down. But that is the path to an ice-cold plunge.

The waves are noisy and ominous and close.

They demand your attention.

The horizon is silent and distant.

But it's there you find your balance.

The crises are clamorous. But look up. Beyond your circumstance. See the always-level, never-changing Jesus. Eyes on him.

Be brutally honest about what's distracting you. World events? Temptations? Other people? Workplace tension? Politics? You can't fight those waves. They are relentless. They are beyond your control. So stop staring at them. Look beyond them to Jesus.

How? Personally, I have found prayer in bed the moment I wake up to be crucial for my focus for the rest of the day. The instant I'm awake, before I pick up my phone, before I make coffee, often before I even open my eyes, I lie there and pray through the Lord's Prayer from memory. Often I pray through the Fruit of the Spirit passage in Galatians 5:22-23 or Psalm 23 as well.

Refocusing needs to be constant. Daily. It takes discipline to avoid looking at the stormy weather in your imagination or in the headlines.

Ask yourself: **Am I focused on the storms or on the Savior?**

> And when they climbed into the boat, the wind died down. Then those who were in the boat worshiped him, saying, "Truly you are the Son of God." (Matthew 14:32-33)

Now this is a first for the disciples. They *worshipped* him. Because they saw how he could "calm the roaring seas, the roaring of their waves." Which, you'll remember, Psalm 65 said only *God* can do. And here Jesus is, right in front of them, with that exact power.

He really is **I Am.**

They still don't quite understand exactly how Jesus is the Son of God. They have not suddenly developed deep comprehensive theology. But they know he's someone unique. Special. Divine.

BOSTON, USA
1990

Early morning, March 18. Two thieves disguised as police officers claim to be responding to an alarm at the Isabella Stewart Gardner Museum. The guards who let them in are handcuffed to pipes in the basement and wrapped in duct tape.

Security footage shows the two fake cops methodically removing the museum's most valuable items, including works by Vermeer, Degas, Manet, and others. From 1:48 to 2:45 a.m., thirteen paintings worth about half a billion dollars are stolen. These remain the most valuable stolen objects in the world. It is the most famous art theft in history. The crime is still unsolved.

Among the vanished works is Rembrandt's "The Storm on the Sea of Galilee," based on a different storm described in Mark 4. The museum still displays its empty frame, just as it was found later that morning.

The painting is the rarest of Rembrandt's works—his only seascape. Most artists labor for years before they capture the sea accurately. Rembrandt nailed it on his first try, at 27 years old, and then moved on.

His painting draws you into the drama. You feel the salt spray as a massive wave looms over a small boat. The sailors are terrified. The ship's mast slashes across the painting diagonally, dividing the canvas into two halves: the right side is dark with violent clouds, the left side offers a tiny peak of blue sky.

None of the sailors notice that hint of dawn, though. The storm paralyzes them. This is not a painting of spiritual serenity. This is a painting of sheer terror.

You can barely see Jesus in the dark among the terrified sailors. He has not yet commanded the storm to stop. Of course, the original 17th-century viewers of the painting knew the familiar story. The wind and waves will soon be stilled. But this is *one split second* before that. All still seems lost. They ask Jesus, "Teacher, don't you care if we drown?"

The people in the painting are feeling what you may be experiencing right now. Super-sized swells swamp the boat. You try to believe Jesus is with you. *But then why isn't he doing something?*

The unsolved theft of the Rembrandt painting can serve as a metaphor for all life's storms. Justice may be elusive. Questions remain unanswered. Storms rage on.

But one day, Jesus will calm every storm. Every injustice. Every disease. Every grieving heart.

"He will wipe every tear from their eyes. There will be no more death or mourning or crying or pain, for the old order of things has passed away." (Revelation 21:4)

Look: See that upper corner of Rembrandt's painting? There's a light ahead.

Watch a short video for this chapter filmed on location

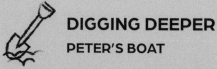

DIGGING DEEPER
PETER'S BOAT

January 24, 1986. A misty rain breaks a long drought at Nof Ginosar kibbutz on the shore of Galilee. On an early morning sail, two brothers see something curious poking up from the mud. They can't believe their eyes: It looks like an ancient boat. At this exact moment, they look up and see a double rainbow.

They immediately contact famous marine archaeologist Dr. Kurt Raveh and Texas A&M biblical archaeology professor Dr. Shelley Wachsman, who rush to the scene. Three independent precision carbon-14 tests confirm their opinion: The brothers have found an intact wooden fishing vessel from the time of Christ—the very kind Jesus and his disciples fished in. It had been covered with mud, which preserved it to an amazing degree. Radiocarbon tests date the wood to 40 BC. Pottery found within the ship dates to nearly AD 50, so this boat was used for over a century—including during the life of Christ. Peter may not have used this boat—there's no way to know—but he certainly saw it. The ship's now housed in a building at the kibbutz, where I could see it, too.

This incredibly rare find helps us picture what Peter's boat was probably like—a 27-foot long, flat-bottom, shallow-drafted boat designed to get close to shore while fishing. It was initially made of cedar planks and oak pegs but later repaired with ten other types of wood. There was a mast for sailing and four rowing positions.

One curious detail about this boat: It can comfortably seat about... *twelve people*.

3
WHEN JESUS GETS CONFUSING
JOHN 6:25–69

ROME
1942

The archaeologists hand-picked by the pope work in silence and secrecy far beneath the crowds visiting St. Peter's Basilica. Soon, they unearth another tomb. This one bears an inscription dated to AD 180:

"Peter, pray to Christ Jesus for the holy Christian men buried near your body."

The tomb of Peter must be nearby!

Excavating at a rapid clip now, they find a red wall and twin pillars matching the ancient description of Peter's small shrine. It's the right age, too, built around AD 160 (this is certain because bricks are found stamped with the date). This must be it, the shrine buried by Constantine and thought lost forever. The archaeologists launch into a single-minded search for Peter's coffin, digging into the earth beneath the shrine, even tossing aside bones they deem insignificant.

Meanwhile, a priest assigned to oversee the excavation, Ludwig Kaas, is horrified at what he sees as disrespect for the dead. Kaas descends into the dimly lit tombs each night with a young member of the facilities crew to find any stray skeletons that may have emerged during the day's digging. The priest hopes to ensure no bones are mixed with the mounds of dirt and accidentally thrown out. Whenever he finds human remains, he places them in special wooden boxes and stores them for reburial.[16]

He doesn't know it yet, but he has saved Peter's bones from being lost forever.

CAPERNAUM, SEA OF GALILEE
PRESENT DAY

I am standing inside a spaceship.

Well, it looks like a spaceship. It's a flying saucer-shaped, glass-bottomed church on the shore of the Sea of Galilee. Why would anyone build a glass-bottom church? In 1968, before this church was built, archaeologists made an astonishing discovery here.

They found Simon Peter's house.

As in, the very house in the Bible where Jesus heals Peter's mother-in-law, the very place where guys eager to get their paralyzed friend to Jesus ripped apart the roof and lowered their buddy down on ropes. That house.

Scholars suspected it was here based on ancient descriptions in Byzantine chronicles, so they meticulously removed layer after layer of debris, like peeling away the skin of an onion. Here's what they found, from top to bottom:

Layer 1: In the fifth century, a beautiful eight-sided church was built over a pre-existing structure. Octagonal churches like that usually marked important sacred sites.

Layer 2: Underneath that church was an older place of worship, a converted house, colorfully painted in floral designs.

Layer 3: Beneath that church was a house that had been remodeled dramatically immediately following AD 30. The main room was plastered. The house's pottery switched from pots and bowls to storage jars and oil lamps, indicating it was no longer used as a private home but a space for assembly. More than a hundred pieces of graffiti had been scratched into the walls, lines like "Lord Jesus Christ, help your servant" and "Christ have mercy." There were etchings of small crosses and a boat. The name Peter was found several times.

Layer 4: Below that was the original house on the site, built in the early first century. It was larger than most homes in the neighborhood but still very simple, with a roof of earth and straw. Picture a small ranch-style house with rooms clustered around two courtyards.

Based on this evidence, scientific dating, and written records, experts concluded this was the house of Simon Peter.

Since their discovery, that unique glass-bottomed church was built. So if you get distracted during the sermon, you can

Ruins of Peter's house and later ancient churches beneath the modern church in Capernaum

look beneath your feet at a 2,000-year-old house in which Jesus probably lived, taught, and healed.

Pretty cool.

I stroll down the steps and out of the church. About 30 yards to my left is the lake. To my right are the ruins of the old synagogue, about the same distance away. I turn right, walk over, and sit along the walls, just where villagers would have listened to the Sabbath sermons. The black rock foundations of this place are from Peter's time.

So there's no doubt. This is the spot where Jesus Christ gave his final sermon in the city, the sermon that outraged the crowds so much that even many of his own disciples walked out on him.

This was the day Jesus got canceled.

Does anything about Christianity put you off? Ever find yourself puzzled by things Jesus said? (Raising my hand right now.)

Same with his first followers.

Sometimes, Jesus seems super cool to follow—all that teaching about loving others and not judging people. Other times, not so much. Other times, Jesus is confusing.

Claiming he is The Way, the only way, to eternal life?

Claiming that by his blood, we are saved? What does that even mean?

That stuff is harder for most people to take than the "love one another" material.

That stuff loses him followers.

From the start.

The Gospel of John chapter 6 describes what happened that day.

What a week Jesus was wrapping up. Two days earlier, he had miraculously fed 5,000 with a few scraps. The day before, he had calmed a storm. Now as Sabbath approaches, the Capernaum crowds try to goad him into another lunch miracle. But Jesus wants to preach first, like a youth pastor doing his talk before pizza time. The crowds sit down eagerly but soon get restless as he speaks. They don't like what they're hearing. And they want to get out and enjoy the buffet.

But Jesus says, forget bread. *He* is the Bread of Life. That's confusing enough.

Then he says partaking of his flesh and his blood will lead to eternal life. We now understand this as referring to his sacrifice for us on the cross which we remember at communion. But at the time, understandably, his audience shifts nervously in their seats. What is he talking about?

Then he says he came down from heaven. John describes the muttering that rustled through the room. "Wait. Isn't this Jesus, Joseph's son, whose father and mother we know? We *know* he didn't come down from heaven."

> On hearing it, many of his disciples said, "This is a hard teaching. Who can accept it?" ... From this time many of his disciples turned back and no longer followed him. (John 6:60,66)

That sentence has a finality in the original Greek. Follow you? No more.

Sociologist Christian Smith coined the phrase "Moralistic Therapeutic Deism" to describe the actual religious beliefs of many Americans, even many who call themselves Christians.

It's *moralistic* because it defines faith as being a good, moral person.

It's *therapeutic* because it defines the goal of faith as making me happy.

It's *deism* because in this faith God exists somewhere up there, but I don't really want him in my daily life (except to give me good stuff).

Moralistic Therapeutic Deism.

People who believe this might view God as "something like a combination Divine Butler and Cosmic Therapist."[17]

That could describe the religion of those who left Jesus that day. Jesus as, vaguely, the prophet of God? Sure. Jesus helps me get free stuff? Absolutely! Jesus gets specific about his unique God-given mission and makes me uncomfortable about my priorities? Forget it, I'm outta here. For them, he wasn't really Jesus Christ. He was Jesus Caterer.

> "You do not want to leave too, do you?" Jesus asked the Twelve. (John 6:67)

I love Peter's response, I really do.

> Simon Peter answered him, "Lord, to whom shall we go?" (John 6:68a)

Not exactly a ringing endorsement.

Imagine that as a blurb on a book: "Most people have stopped reading this author, but I don't currently know a better alternative."

Peter seems to be implying,

"Leave? We've thought about it.

You know, a lot of the time, we don't get you either.

But—leaving to go... where, exactly?"

Every Christian should memorize his response. Because this is real life.

Like everyone, I suffered trauma. Some of my specific setbacks: My dad died when I was little, after which we lived in poverty, during which a teacher sexually molested me. My mother remarried, but a decade later, my stepdad died of a heart attack. My mom died of Alzheimer's after we cared for her in our home. There's a list.

People have asked me, "René, how did all that not destroy your faith?" I guess they mean, how could I not question God or get mad at God? Well, of course, I questioned God, and of course, I got mad at God.

But—leave? Leave to go where, exactly?

Look. Tough times will happen, whether you're in the faith or outside the faith. So why not stay where you are going to get support, where you are going to hear inspiring words, where you are going to be assured that God loves you and can redeem your suffering, where you can find camaraderie with other struggling, doubting, suffering, imperfect, flawed, but sincere Jesus-followers?

Leave? Sure, I've thought about it. *But to whom shall I go?*

To whom could Peter have gone?

Peter had versions of the same alternatives we have today.

There's Caesar.
Force. Military might. But imagine a world influenced only by the Roman Empire, devoid of any of Jesus' teachings. Love your enemies? More like, stab your enemies in the back. Sure, there were alternatives to Caesar. The revolutionaries. But they were just substituting their violence for his.

There's political power.
Several groups were striving for power in Peter's day: The Zealots, who were often violent activists; the Herodian collaborators, who adopted many Roman customs and values; the high priests, who combined religion with political power. Historically speaking, none of them lasted.

There's legalistic religion.
Emphasizing ritual and rules rather than the grace-motivated gospel of Jesus. Religious micro-management may make you feel secure, but it drains your joy.

There's Stoicism.
One of the most dominant philosophies in Peter's time, this emphasized willpower, self-control. Great as far as it goes. But if you're honest, you know willpower is not always enough.

There's hedonism.
The main rival of Stoicism. *Seek pleasure. Avoid pain.* In classical hedonism, pleasures must be kept modest, but we all know how that goes. Pleasure quickly becomes a manic god demanding to be served at all times.

There's magical thinking.
If I do the right rituals, I'll have prosperity. Big in Peter's time. Still popular today. Just manifest hard enough, do the ritual, smudge the sage, harness the crystal, and you'll get what you want. Crystals are pretty and sage smells great, but we all know the truth: No matter the ritual, suffering is inevitable. Rituals put a lot of pressure on you. Just like many forms of religion, they are performative, based on you getting it just right.

There's following your own star.
Do whatever you want. But can you imagine a world where everyone did this at every level? Pure chaos. Plus, how does this challenge any of your assumptions? Unless someone demonstrably wiser than you is speaking truth to you, you'll operate as if your ideas, conclusions, and impulses are always right. Not only will this lead you to ruin, but you will also be no fun at parties.

Yes, there are alternatives. But is there a better one than Jesus?

Then Peter moves to his primary reason for sticking with Jesus:

"You have the words of eternal life." (John 6:68b)

It's revealing to note what he did *not* say.

He did not say, "Lord, you do the miracles. Lord, when we're hungry, you make us food." In fact, we discover many of those who left had been following Jesus only because they liked the free food and fine wine. When the tap was turned off, they took off.

No, Peter likes the *words*.

Think about this. You and I were not able to walk with Jesus in person or see his miracles in person, but what Peter valued most—Christ's words—is what we still have today.

Peter also does not say, "Lord, we *understand* every word! We totally get it!" Because Jesus leaves a lot of puzzling statements just hanging in midair. But Peter knows those words are worth puzzling over, worth peering into and pondering.

"You have the words of eternal life."

Words like the ones he had heard that very day. Words like:

> "I am the bread of life. Whoever comes to me will never go hungry, and whoever believes in me will never be thirsty."
> (John 6:35)

Jesus is not just *offering* bread. He *is* the bread. He is life. He is satisfaction.

Words like:

> "...everyone who looks to the Son and believes in him shall have eternal life, and I will raise them up at the last day."
> (John 6:40b)

Jesus' earth-shattering claim here is that our eternal life is not based on our performance but on the simplest, child-like faith imaginable. It's accessible to anyone. Look to him and believe.

Then here's the most important thing Simon Peter says.

> "We have come to believe and know that you are the Christ, the Son of the living God." (John 6:69 WEB)

Love that. *We have come to believe.* In 12-step groups, step two begins with the phrase "we came to believe" because sobriety is a process. You need to be patient and let it unfold.

Same with faith.

Peter and his friends followed first. Tagged along. Watched and listened and considered and served. And then they *came to believe.* They *developed* faith in Jesus *as* they *walked with* Jesus.

They were not cynical skeptics.
They were not unthinking fanatics.
They were careful followers.
That's biblical faith.

Even when confused, they were willing to keep following to see where it might lead.

The invitation of Jesus is to "follow me," not "have no further questions about me." There are always unanswered questions. But consider this: Where in life are there *not* unanswered questions?

> "We have come to believe and know that you are the Christ, the Son of the living God."

Simon Peter will affirm that in detail a little later on. He is saying, "We don't always *get* you. But we *trust* you."

Sometimes after church services people come up to tell me they're new believers. But one day, a guy threw me a curveball. He walked up and confessed, "Rene, I am now an unbeliever."

I said, "Well... define that for me." (Always a good tip when you're stumped by what someone just told you. "Define that." Buys you time.)

He answered, "Well, I do believe in Jesus, but I also have all these doubts."

I turned to a verse in Mark where a man says to Christ, "I do believe; help my unbelief!" (Mark 9:24) And Jesus *commends* him for his faith. I asked the man, "Can you pray that prayer? 'Lord, I believe—but help my unbelief?'" He said, "That's an awesome prayer, that describes me exactly!"

I said, "Then you have the faith Jesus commended. Because that's real life right there: 'I believe—but I have questions.' Jesus says, 'Great, you're just the kind of honest person I'm looking for.'"

That man represents a lot of people I see in my church and, I suspect, any church. Intrigued by Jesus. But uncertain about committing themselves to "become Christians," reluctant to proceed without ironclad proof.

But faith isn't about absolute certainty. It's about believing something's *worth the risk*. If you wait for absolute certainty, you'll never do anything.

In college, I was influenced by the Danish philosopher Søren Kierkegaard, a brilliant man who found he could argue for and against Christianity. Attracted to it. Yet questioned it.

Finally, he realized that, as with any critical decision, there comes a "leap of faith." (That's how his idea is often summarized in English, though the phrase that more accurately represents his thinking is a "leap *into* faith.")

He took the leap. Months later, he remembered that decisive moment and wrote in his journal, **"The greatest danger is not to take the risk."**

One curse of our modern age is that we're growing exponentially in our knowledge—yet shrinking in our ability to act decisively. We often feel that with just a little bit more information, we'd have all the evidence and *then*, finally, could make a decision.

You don't have to know it all.
You don't have to understand every page of the Bible.
You don't have to agree with everything your pastor says.
You don't have to have all your theological questions answered.
You just have to decide how to respond to Jesus' invitation. *Follow me.*

But biblical faith isn't *blind* faith, either. It isn't about forgetting your questions. It doesn't mean pretending you have no doubts. Because doubts and questions can actually deepen your faith.

In the Bible, "faith" means *trust*. Trust is based on reasonable, compelling evidence and experience.

You put your trust in things every day. Whenever you use a navigation app, you trust it to lead you correctly. When you drive across a bridge, you trust it won't collapse. In any love relationship, you trust that person's love for you.

You trust not because you have thoroughly and scientifically investigated the app, the bridge, or the person and have 100 percent proof of their integrity, and not because you have no more questions, but because you have good enough reasons to trust. To go ahead. To believe your trust will lead you somewhere good.

Blaise Pascal was a scientific prodigy in the 1600s. Centuries ahead of his time, he invented one of the first mechanical calculators and was a staunch defender of the scientific method. He also became a man of strong Christian faith.

Pascal argued that our decisions can be enormously consequential, even though our understanding of all the factors that go into those decisions is *always* limited. While we can learn a lot through research and reason, we are ultimately forced to gamble every time we choose anything.

This is why, he said, it is logical to live as if God exists, and to strive to believe in God. People of faith live demonstrably healthier and more disciplined lives now, and possibly better lives after death, too. If God does not truly exist, people of faith don't really lose anything. If God does exist, they gain immeasurably. But if people choose to live as if God does *not* exist, they lose the advantage of church community and beauty and history in this life, and may lose benefits in the next life too.

Yet, Pascal said, God will not compel faith, because love is never compelled.

> In faith, there is enough light for those who want to believe
> and enough shadows to blind those who don't. – Blaise Pascal

Why doesn't God just give irrefutable evidence that he exists? Pascal's premise: If God became as visible to you as the tree outside your window, then you would have no need for faith. You couldn't help but believe in God. It would be impossible to deny Him! But that's not the sort of relationship God desires. God does not just want you to agree that he *exists*, like you agree that iron atoms exist; God wants you to choose to *love* Him. Love must involve trust. Trust must involve faith.

In an article called "Reconstructing Faith: Christianity in a New World," Tim Keller pointed out how many people raised in the church have been rethinking their previously unquestioned beliefs. This trend has been called "deconstruction."[18]

Some see deconstruction as entirely negative. But Keller says if deconstruction means honestly analyzing your faith, rejecting false assumptions and warped teachings, and approaching Jesus on his own terms, then it is helpful.

In fact, that is precisely what Jesus forced his hearers in that Capernaum synagogue to do. That was the point. His challenging words peeled back the layers of their motivations and preconceptions. Peter and the other disciples were forced to examine why they followed Jesus. Was it because he was their lucky rabbit's foot? Was he just their ticket to the premium lounge, the one with free food and complimentary beverages?

In other words: Was it about them? Or was it about him?

Peter still had questions. You'll see them come up as our story unfolds. **But he chose to see if some of those questions might be answered as he followed.**

It's not that there are no further mysteries—who would want a life without mystery? It's that there are reasons to keep following Jesus—one step at a time, one lesson at a time, one day at a time.

Even if, as Peter is about to experience, Jesus takes you straight to the gates of hell.

Watch a short video for this chapter filmed on location

DIGGING DEEPER
PETER'S NEIGHBORHOOD

The Galilee region is beautiful. Visitors are often surprised at how little development there is here compared to the skyscrapers of Tel Aviv, and like to imagine it was rural in Peter's time too. But Galilee was much more developed then than it is now.

Capernaum means "Comfortville," and it fits. The first-century writer Josephus rapturously described it this way:

> "Skirting the lake lies a region whose natural properties and beauty are remarkable. There is not a plant that its fertile soil refuses to produce, and its cultivators grow every species ... Its nature is wonderful, as is its beauty ... It supplies people with grapes and figs continually for ten months of the year. Besides the good temperature of the air, it is also watered from a most fertile fountain. The people of that country call it Capharnaum..."

> "Moreover, the cities here are very thick, and the many villages there are everywhere, so full of people, by the richness of their soil, that the very least of them contain above fifteen thousand inhabitants."*

Although near the Mediterranean, Galilee has a subtropical climate. Among the largest farms are banana, papaya, and mango orchards.

To get the feel of Galilee in the first century, imagine California in the booming 1960s—only with a climate and geology a little more like Hawaii. As in the Hawaiian islands, the oldest structures here are usually made from the plentiful black lava rock.

* *The Jewish War* 3:516-521, translation by H. St. J. Thackeray in Vol. II of *Josephus* [London: William Heinemann, 1927], in the *Loeb Classical Library* series

4
WHEN PANIC ATTACKS
MATTHEW 16:13–17:5

ROME
1942

World War II rages throughout Europe. Hundreds of Allied planes drop their bombs on Rome. The tunnel walls of the secret excavation shiver with each blast, pebbles sprinkling onto archaeologists' helmets as they search desperately for Peter's grave.

Digging for what they believe will be a bronze casket, they peel back the layers of marble and brick covering the ancient shrine but have not yet found anything resembling a coffin.

Then they discover a small hole near the very base of the red wall, as if someone had burrowed directly into the ground beneath the shrine. In that hole, they find bones.

The pope is summoned, and, though he is perplexed to find Peter's bones laid directly in the dirt instead of inside his shrine, he and the team conclude they have finally uncovered Peter's remains.

The bones are placed in lead-lined boxes at the pope's direction and moved to his apartment, where they will remain hidden for many years. At his express command, "This find is to be kept absolutely secret."[19]

His instructions will not be obeyed.

This is the most personal chapter of the book for me.

One day, after three years as pastor at Twin Lakes Church, I drove home from the office, threw myself on the bed, and told my wife Laurie, "I hate my job. I hate my life." There was so much church debt, so many negative letters, so little progress, so much to do that I was losing hope.

A little later, I was sitting on our couch and suddenly experienced sharp chest pains. I could hardly breathe. I had tunnel vision. My head was splitting. Laurie thought I was having a stroke or heart attack and rushed me to the emergency room. A doctor connected me to a bewildering array of diagnostic machines, drew blood, analyzed results, and then told me I was not, in fact, dying.

I was having a significant anxiety attack—the first of several. I was crippled by panic.

Anxiety and panic attacks are on the rise today—at greater levels than ever before. One effect of these attacks is a loss of power to believe that any good awaits you. Pessimism fogs your brain like a cloud.

What's the answer to these deep feelings of inferiority and apprehension?

While recuperating, I rigorously followed my doctor's advice to rest and to exercise. I was helped by prescribed medication. I read every book on panic and anxiety that I could get my hands on. I got amazing help from skilled, licensed therapists. I searched the Bible for every verse on the topic.

I found lots of great verses. But it was one Bible story, one verse, one idea that gave me the most comfort of all. It's an encounter between Jesus and Peter.

At first, I couldn't understand why it encouraged me so much. After all, it has nothing to do with panic. Then I visited the spot where it happened. And discovered it was Panic Central.

In the winter before his death on the cross, Jesus takes his disciples on a 30-mile road trip, far from their familiar fishing grounds, northward into thoroughly pagan territory devoted to the worship of the wildest of the pagan gods, Pan, the god of the groves and the goats. And panic.

I've driven the route myself several times. If you follow the Jordan River north from Galilee, the road rises sharply. The landscape changes. The peak of Mount Hermon comes into view. At 9,000 feet above sea level, Hermon is the highest mountain in Israel and the source of the Jordan River. Soon waterfalls thunder over cliffs beside the road. The sparse forests become lush as a jungle. In Jesus' day, these woods hid bears, wolves, and leopards.

Then you see it—the astonishing source of the river.

The Jordan doesn't start humbly like your average waterway, with creeks and streams mildly trickling together, but with a dramatic flourish. As you emerge from the woods in the foothills of Mount Hermon, a giant sheer cliff looms above you, over 100 feet tall and 500 feet wide. A gaping cavern opens within it. Beneath the cave gushes ice-cold spring water.

The river has been gestating slowly in the darkness of the mountain's womb, innumerable tiny fissures collecting rain and snow until here it explodes into birth. In Jesus' era, the water flowed right out of the cavern, though falling rocks from several later earthquakes blocked the cave and the water now emerges more slowly in front of the cliff. Even so, it still creates a sparkling green oasis of life. When the disciples visited, the cliff face also bristled with stone temples and shrines carved for pagan gods and for dictators claiming divinity.

The Dark Cave
Despite its natural beauty, this must have been a place of significant stress for any first-century Jewish man like Peter, for five good reasons:

1. Canaanite Baal worship.
For centuries, this area was associated with the fertility god of the ancient Canaanites, Baal, long opposed by the Israelites.

2. Greek Pan worship.
Alexander the Great built a temple here for Pan, naming the area "Paneas." Pan was the god of the wild, of goats and hunting and sexual urges. He looked like our traditional images of the devil, with horns, goat-like hooves, his tongue always stuck out in a suggestive leer like some eighties heavy metal rock star.

Pan was said to have the power to make people flee in unreasoning fear, which is why we get our word "panic" from his name. Roman soldiers on their way to besiege Jerusalem in AD 70 stopped here and prayed for Pan to fill their enemies with panic. You could call this the Temple of Panic, where reason gave way to wildness.

3. Roman emperor worship.

When the brutal King Herod the Great was given this territory by Caesar Augustus, he built a white marble temple here, worshipping the emperor as a god.

4. Roman wealth and oppression.

When Herod died, his son Philip spectacularly redeveloped the city, building a palace and a resort, changing its name to Caesarea Philippi. It became the go-to R&R destination for Roman soldiers. They could relax in the spa and visit the temple prostitutes. And guess whose taxes paid for all that luxury? The oppressed Jews.

5. The Gates of Hades.

The pagans feared and revered this as a gate to the shadowy underworld called Hades. They believed the fertility gods spent the dry season there and had to be reawakened with annual rituals featuring goat sacrifices and prostitution.

> So. Wow.
> Baal. Pan. Caesar.
> Pagan worship. Emperor worship.
> Prostitution. Oppression. Superstition.
> The underworld. The army.

In Jesus' day, this was more than just a strange place. It represented the entire pagan Gentile world, the vast system that opposed the true God and oppressed the people. Every detail must have infuriated and disgusted his disciples. It was blasphemous. It was oppressive.

And in this unlikely spot, Jesus asks them a question. It's the question his entire ministry had been leading toward. It's the same question he eventually asks every one of us.

"*Who do you say I am?*"

For three years, Jesus has been slowly revealing his identity through words and deeds. Now, he wants to know what they think.

In their answer, the disciples seem to hedge their bets: "Well, some people think you're John the Baptist, others think you're Elijah, still others Jeremiah, or some other prophet." It's like when I used to guess answers to math problems when called on in class: "It's… 238. Or 457. Or 5," hoping for a sign from the teacher that I was getting close.

But what about *you*, says Jesus. Who do *you* say I am?

Here it comes.

> Simon Peter answered, "You are the Messiah, the Son of the living God." (Matthew 16:16)

The word "Messiah" literally means "anointed One." It's the Hebrew word for any prophet, priest, or king anointed by God for a special purpose. "Christ" is simply the Greek word for "anointed." Christ was not Jesus' last name (and his middle initial is not H). Christ is a title; it means "Messiah."

The Hebrew Scriptures prophesied that one day God would send THE Messiah—prophet, priest, and king all rolled into one. This Messiah was called "the Son of God," the final Anointed One who would rescue Israel from oppression and kick off a reign of peace and prosperity.

Peter says, *I think that's you.*

Jesus replied, "Blessed are you, Simon son of Jonah, for this was not revealed to you by flesh and blood, but by my Father in heaven." (Matthew 16:17)

Seems to me Jesus is saying something like, *Wow. I know YOU did not come up with that one on your own.* And if you've been following Peter's story, you know exactly what Jesus means. If Peter took a personality test, it would not come back with "You are a slow-processing yet perceptive analyst who carefully weighs his words." Peter just blurts it out. But this time his blurt is right. Jesus *is* The Messiah.

Then here's the part that encouraged me in my times of panic. After Peter correctly identifies *Jesus*, Jesus correctly identifies *Peter*.

"And I tell you that you are Peter, and on this rock I will build my church, and the gates of Hades will not overcome it." (Matthew 16:18)

This is what I memorized and meditated on during that dark night of my own soul. I really wanted to do great things for God and for humanity, to be part of what Jesus was doing. Yet there were so many giant obstacles and I had so many giant weaknesses that I became convinced I was too flawed, too weak, too ordinary.

Here, in this one verse, I found three truths that have brought me such hope and stability.

1. Jesus builds his church with common material.
Aren't you inspired by the fact that Jesus chose a foot-in-mouth, failure-prone guy like Simon Peter to lead the early

church? That means he can use you and me, too. You don't have to be a flawless superstar.

When he says, "You are Peter, and on this rock," Jesus is making a pun on Simon's nickname. You can't tell in English, but in the original Greek language, both the name *Petros* and the word for rock, *petra*, are from the same root. They both mean rock. Jesus probably spoke in Aramaic, which also has the same word for both: *Kepha*.

Peter = The Rock.[20] Dwayne Johnson was not the first person to be nicknamed The Rock.

Jesus is making a pun. *I gave you a nickname. The Rock. And upon this rock, I will build my church.*

Plus, remember, this is happening near a gigantic rock, so it's a triple wordplay. I think this is why Jesus brought them specifically here. He is saying, *What I build on the rock called Rocky will outlast anything on that rock.*

Have you noticed how God often gives new names to people? For example, Abram (which means "great father") became Abraham ("father of many"). At the time of his name change, Abraham was childless! It's not a *recognition*. It's a *promise*.

Same here. Peter was the same impetuous, unstable, inconsistent man he was a moment before. But Jesus knows something. Peter will grow into his name.

Do you let Jesus correctly identify you?
He calls you family. (Matthew 12:49)
He calls you beloved. (John 13:34)
He calls you friend. (John 15:15)
He calls you chosen. (John 15:16)
He calls you the salt of the earth. (Matthew 5:13)
He calls you the light of the world. (Matthew 5:14)

Don't feel like it's true? Keep listening. You'll grow into it.

2. Jesus builds it, not me.
"I will build my church."

Just let that soak in. *He* builds it.

Many years later, Peter wrote a letter to the early Christians. He tells them,

> "And you also are living stones that God is building..."
> (1 Peter 2:5)

You also! What Jesus saw in Peter is true of us all. See the beauty of this? I'm a stone. He's the stonemason. I'm a chess piece. He's the chess master. I don't have to know all the answers. I can trust there's a plan.

So when I feel tired, that's okay. When I feel confused, that's okay too. He's in charge. He is not depending on my brilliance or strength.

3. Jesus' work is built to last.

> "... and the gates of Hades will not overcome it." (Matthew 16:18)

I imagine Jesus gesturing to Pan's shrine, which looked like massive gates leading into the cavern. The disciples look up and they see temples clad in white marble and crowded with well-trained soldiers from the most enormous army the world had ever seen, financed by the wealthiest empire the world had ever seen. Then they look back at their little gang.

Hades has all that. Heaven has these twelve yokels.

Yet those gates to the underworld at Caesarea Philippi crumbled into ruin after about AD 600, while the movement Jesus started has thrived for millennia.

The gates of Hades did not overcome it.

I think of the Christian movement in China. During the Cultural Revolution, churches were closed, Bibles were burned, crosses were destroyed, and many Christian believers were sent to prisons or labor camps.

When the country reopened, what had happened to the Christians there—after decades of effort to completely wipe them out? You'd be astonished if I told you their numbers had stayed the same. You'd call it a miracle if I told you they had doubled. Yet most scholars estimate that the Christian population there increased by a factor of 50!

And it keeps growing. Boston University scholar Daryl Ireland explained his extensive research in a 2023 interview: "Over the last 40 years, Christianity has grown faster in China than any other place in the world. It's gone from approximately 1 million Christians to around 100 million. This is just an incredible explosion."[21]

If the growth of Christians in China continues at this rate, within one or two decades, there will be more Christians there than in the U.S.

"...and the gates of Hades will not overcome it."

For you, the gates of Hades may not look like a repressive government. It may look like a lump, a pain, a shadow on an MRI, a final text message, the end of the business, the end of the marriage, the end of a job, the end of the dream. The underworld.

Jesus says no. That is not the end. Hades will not prevail. He will.

Are you ready for one of the most controversial verses in Scripture? Jesus tells Peter,

> "I will give you the keys of the kingdom of heaven. Whatever you bind on earth will be bound in heaven, and whatever you loose on earth will be loosed in heaven." (Matthew 16:19)

Battles have been waged over how to read this verse. Catholics see it as a reference to papal authority. Many Protestants think Jesus is referring to the confession of Peter.

Here's my take on this (and if you disagree, just email razi.fisherman@fishsauce.com).

First, this doesn't mean Peter will stand forever at the gates of heaven with keys and a list, deciding who gets in and who stays out, like in a million jokes.

Although those are funny. Like: A Catholic arrives at the pearly gates. Peter says, "Please proceed to your room in the heavenly mansion, door 31, and sneak past door 12." Then a Presbyterian shows up. "Your place," says St. Peter, "is down the hall, door 143, and please sneak past door 12." A Pentecostal gets there next, and Peter tells him, "Your heavenly room is behind door 43. But go quietly past number 12."

The Pentecostal says, "It's so hard for us to be quiet, why do I have to sneak past door 12?" Peter says, "Well, those are the Baptists. They think they're the only ones here."

Ba-dum-BUM.

But seriously. Peter is not standing at the gates judging. Jesus is. And he says there's a simple way in:

"For my Father's will is that everyone who looks to the Son and believes in him shall have eternal life, and I will raise them up at the last day." (John 6:40)

That's a promise.

So what does this verse mean?

Well, the best way to explain hard-to-understand Bible verses is to look for explanations within the Bible itself. Is this a callback to another Scripture? Turns out Jesus is quoting a line from Isaiah 22, where God tells the prophet Isaiah to fire the prideful palace administrator, Shebna, and replace him with a more noble man named Eliakim. Here's how God describes what is about to happen:

> "I will clothe him with your robe and fasten your sash around him and hand your authority over to him ... I will place on his shoulder the key to the house of David; what he opens no one can shut, and what he shuts no one can open."
> (Isaiah 22:21,22)

The "house of David" was the royal line that would run all the way to the promised Messiah. The king's chief of staff was said to have the keys to the house. He was not the Messiah or the king; you could call him an executive officer or deputy.[22]

Jesus is using biblical language to *deputize* Peter, just as Isaiah deputized Eliakim. The metaphor of keys is apt. Peter will unlock many doors for people—as we will soon see.

But first, Peter puts his foot in his mouth. Again.

> From that time on Jesus began to show His disciples that He must go to Jerusalem and suffer many things at the hands of the elders, chief priests, and scribes, and that He must be killed and on the third day be raised to life. (Matthew 16:21)

This did not compute.

Jesus has just affirmed that he's the long-awaited ultimate Messiah, the one prophesied to deliver Israel from all oppressors. Not get *killed*.

Peter thinks, maybe Jesus has lost the plot.

> Peter took Him aside and began to rebuke Him. "Far be it from You, Lord!" he said. "This shall never happen to You!" (Matthew 16:22 ESV)

Who can blame him? The Messiah we want is a strongman who punches the bad guys in the mouth—not a humble servant who gets punched in the mouth. Peter expected something like "Captain Israel," a super-powered anti-Roman, leading a revolt like the Maccabean brothers did two centuries before—only this time God's Mega-Messiah would bring a lasting victory.

Pastor Steve Cuss distinguishes between *precious* beliefs and *core* beliefs. He points out that even when Jesus is your most *precious* belief, that is probably not your *deepest* belief. Underneath your love for Jesus is a nest of assumptions that may keep you from really understanding and experiencing Christ fully.

You see this happening here with Simon Peter. Jesus had become his most *precious*, treasured belief. But Peter had even deeper, *core* beliefs.

Peter assumed the key to happiness was political independence. The only way to political independence was for a military Messiah to kick out the Romans. This was the story Peter had been told. It was the story he told himself. These core beliefs were such a part of his identity that he never questioned them, yet they kept Peter from understanding how Jesus was offering a totally different path to peace.

What about you? Your most *precious* belief may be Jesus. But do you have *core* beliefs, from your culture or your childhood or your church, that short-circuit your understanding of Jesus?

To discover your core beliefs, ask, "What is the story I tell myself?" Maybe you tell yourself that you must perform to earn the favor of God and others. Maybe you tell yourself you'll never change. Maybe you believe that bad things don't happen to good Christian people. Maybe you think fame or money or looks or pleasure are keys to happiness. Maybe you imagine that if only your children were better, then you'd be happy. Even though you love Jesus, core beliefs like this prevent you from fully experiencing and understanding Christ.

Following Jesus involves letting him realign your core beliefs with his revolutionary truth.

Just as Jesus is about to realign Peter— rather memorably.

> But Jesus turned and said to Peter, "Get behind Me, Satan! You are a stumbling block to Me. For you do not have in mind the things of God, but the things of men." (Matthew 16:23)

Peter must be thinking, "Two minutes ago I was the Rock, now I'm Satan?" Why would Jesus call him that? Seems pretty harsh.

It's because Peter is reiterating Christ's first temptation in the wilderness, when Satan offered him "all the kingdoms of the world and their splendor" without any suffering. All the power, all the glory, no cross, no cost.

At the end of that temptation, it says Satan left him "until an opportune time." (Luke 4:13). Here, Jesus recognizes the sinister source of that same temptation, though it comes through the sincere voice of an ally.

How often do we, as followers of Christ, fail to recognize the Satanic origin of that same idea? "If we could only grab power and force people to do the right thing, then the world would be a better place!" Every time in history we Christians have made this mistake it's been Satanic; it has brought injustice and sorrow. Too often we do not have in mind the ways of God but the ways of men.

Peter had listened to Jesus talk about this new way, this new kind of kingdom for years. In fact, "kingdom" was Jesus Christ's major theme, his favorite word. Just to put into perspective how much Jesus loved this word: He used the word "salvation" 10 times. He used the word "church" three times. He used the words "Taylor Swift" zero times. Jesus used the word "kingdom" 100 times.

But Jesus did not just mean a religious version of the same old politics and armies. **This kingdom is different.**

Jesus says things like, "The kingdom of God ... does not come in such a way as to be seen ... the kingdom of God is within you." (Luke 17:20-21) This kingdom doesn't have a visible capital or castle or cavalry. He says it's like a seed, or like yeast, or like a pearl. It's received like a child, ruled like a servant. There's a smallness, a meekness, an innocence about it.

Peter and the rest of the oppressed people expected the Messiah to just have smarter soldiers and sharper spears than Caesar. But Jesus says, no, we're playing a whole different game. The kingdoms of this world? They're about pride and threats and self-promotion. The kingdom of heaven? Instead of pride, humility. Instead of threats, blessing. Instead of self-promotion, self-sacrifice.

There's an invitation here. Are you tired of the kingdoms of this world? Are you tired of the way they operate? Are you tired of cutthroat politics, the brutality, the division, the infighting, the insults, the power plays, the lies, the manipulations, the preening, self-satisfied rulers? Jesus says, "Well, then do I have an invitation for you."

You can be part of a new kind of kingdom.

When you bless instead of curse, when you forgive instead of hate, when you love instead of ignore, characteristics of Christ's kingdom are manifest on this earth. One day Messiah will restore it fully. In the meantime, we can live our lives as a preview of that day, as ambassadors of the one truly revolutionary kingdom.

While in the Galilee region, I met a remarkable woman named Rula Mansour. She has a PhD from Oxford. She was the Deputy Public Prosecutor for Nazareth. She's an Arab Palestinian Christian Israeli citizen. And now she is in full-time Christian ministry, having started the Nazareth Center for Peace Studies.

She grew up watching the cycles of war and violence in the Middle East. That led her to study how Jesus taught his disciples to represent a new kind of kingdom. Not of the sword. But of love.

Rula says, "Our mission involves being sent into the world to love, to serve, to heal, to save and to free, presenting a counterculture. We fight revenge through mercy, we resist evil with good, and we seek justice on the road to reconciliation."[23]

If that sounds like happy-clappy hippy idealism, Rula insists, "It's not about vague intentions or lofty convictions; it's about practical, consistent practices, a lifestyle that, when faithfully followed, can shape us into peacemakers and free us from the destructive cycles of anger and revenge."

Following her lead, several Palestinian churches in Israel have encouraged their members to open their homes to provide shelter and assistance for needy families, whether Jewish or Palestinian.

That is the Jesus way.

The kingdom of heaven is not just a rebranding of the kingdoms of this world. It's something entirely different on every level.

The Dutch pastor Kornelius Miskotte taught secret Bible study groups during the Nazi occupation of his country. He called Jesus "the ultimate Saboteur." But not through violence. Through holiness. When we live the Jesus way, we are part of God's long, slow sabotage of the world's destructive value system—starting with ourselves. Biblical holiness is not living in some frightened cocoon of throwbacks unable to cope with modern life. It's unrushed resistance. It's subtle sabotage. It's the beautiful alternative. When we bless and pray and respect and love, we are subverting the violence, the sexual objectification, the hedonism, the obsession with power that dominates all this world's kingdoms.

But Simon Peter doesn't get that yet. He doesn't want a suffering servant Savior. He wants a sword-wielding, smiting Savior.

Peter is right about the *who* of Jesus.
Peter is wrong about the *way* of Jesus.

How about you?
We also live in a time when more and more people are joining religious identity with nationalist militarism. They justify using force and dirty politics to achieve "good" ends. But this is not the kind of Messiah that Jesus is.

The stakes are actually much higher than winning an election for a few years of influence. If we push ungodly methods as if they were endorsed by Jesus, we may warp what others perceive "Christianity" to mean—for generations to come.

That is why Jesus says, "Get behind me, Satan."

I love that both of these successive sayings are from Peter's mouth. In five verses, he nails it, aaaaand he spouts ignorant heresy.

To me, that's what makes these gospel stories clearly actual recollections. If you were going to invent the beginning of some new religion, and you, as Peter, wanted to platform yourself as the hand-picked successor to the beloved leader, and you're trying to create your legend, enhance your credibility, highlight your abilities, you definitely would not make yourself out as dense as Peter comes across. You'd paint yourself as so quick to understand what the Master is trying to teach that people would look at one another and whisper, "Such insight!"

Instead, after getting one thing right, Peter promptly takes a header right back into the pavement. Bam!

He's up, he's down.
He floats; he sinks.
He's wise; he's dense.

Yet Jesus not only lets this very flawed follower tag along; Jesus promotes him to be his chief of staff!

See why this story calmed me in my own days of anxiety?

Like me, you may feel like a little pebble, unimportant. The world's evil ways may seem to loom large, far greater than the mild efforts of Christ-followers like you. But Jesus promises: The powers of this world will not be able to stand against what he is doing through you and many others like you.

There's a post-credits scene to this story. A plot twist. A sneak peek.

Six days later, Jesus takes Peter, James, and John to the top of a very high mountain. It's not identified in the text, but I suspect it was Mount Hermon. There, Jesus is transfigured: He begins to shine with bright light. Then the disciples see Moses and Elijah standing with him! Talking with Jesus! Jesus is giving them a glimpse of his heavenly glory!

So much to say here, but we're focused on Peter, so let's look at his response.

How much would you give to have been a fly on the wall that day, just to listen as Moses, Elijah, and Jesus chat? Well, guess what Peter does? He interrupts. Yes. He interrupts Jesus, Moses, and Elijah. Clears his throat: *Ahem.*

> Peter said to Jesus, "Rabbi, it is good for us to be here. Let us put up three shelters—one for you, one for Moses and one for Elijah." (Mark 9:5)

Mark adds,

> He said this because he didn't really know what else to say. (Mark 9:6a NLT)

Now I love that. Peter didn't know what to say. So ... he opened his mouth.

"How about some huts?!"

Maybe Peter was just starstruck.

I understand because I have said some idiotic things when faced with celebrities. Once I rode in an elevator with a very famous pastor as he was about to speak to a large conference I was attending.

I couldn't believe it, "I am in the elevator with Famous Celebrity Pastor." I got Simon Syndrome. I did not know what to say, so I opened my mouth.

First I wanted to say, "good luck!" but then I checked myself because I thought maybe luck sounded too unspiritual so I considered "hope it goes well!" but then I thought "hope" wasn't strong enough and I should probably say something about God and then the elevator doors were opening and Famous Celebrity Pastor was leaving so I had to say something quick and all three options came out jumbled together, blasted at full volume: "GOOD HOPE GOD!!!"

Ding. Doors close. Muzak plays. And I am dying. *"Good hope, God?!"*

Then I realized that was my floor, too. So I pressed the "open" button, and the panels slid back to reveal him still standing there, frozen, with a perplexed look. I thought, "Maybe I short-circuited his brain!" So I pressed "door close" again and just rode the elevator for a while.

Peter seems to always take the high-volume approach to communication: *If I say enough stuff, I'm bound to be right sometimes!* Again I get it. I've ended many days thinking, "I talked too much." Never one time have I thought, "You know, I don't think I said enough words today." Sometimes I find myself in conversations where I start to talk and I cannot stop and even I know I am repeating myself and making no sense I keep prattling on and please someone just step in and interrupt.

Well, things are getting awkward like that on the mountain and God the Father steps in.

> Then a cloud overshadowed them, and a voice from the
> cloud said, "This is my dearly loved Son. Listen to him."
> (Mark 9:7)

How often would God say the same exact thing to me and you? *Uh—stop talking.*

You don't need to post about every event or emotion. Conclusions do not always have to be drawn and platformed. Stop commenting on every single thing that happens. *Listen. To. Jesus.*

Always a good call.

When you're panicked and anxious, listen to Jesus.

When you need assurance you're loved, listen to Jesus.

Especially when you do not know what to say, listen to Jesus.

And remember this: The Prince of Peace is greater than the god of panic.

Oh. But Pan is not done with Peter.

Not yet.

Watch a short video for this chapter filmed on location

DIGGING DEEPER:
THE ALTAR OF PAN

Although we know from literary sources that the temple to Pan dominated the landscape at Caesarea Philippi in Jesus' day, its actual altar was lost for centuries. Then in 2020, a startling discovery was made. Right at the mouth of the cave, archaeologists unearthed an ancient Christian church, one of the earliest ever found. I visited the site in 2022 and saw its beautiful mosaic floors decorated with little crosses. That's an important detail because it shows the cross symbol was already widely understood and used in Christian art at a very early stage. The church was built shortly after Christianity was officially "tolerated" by the Romans.

The most intriguing aspect of the church was its large stone altar, which was dedicated to Pan and adapted for use in the church. The inscription says a traveling merchant from Antioch named Athenaeus funded the altar.

Ancient shrines carved into the Caesarea Philippi cliff

So what's an altar to Pan doing in a Christian church? Excavation director Adi Erlich theorizes that the Christians left the altar in place and repurposed it as a visible demonstration of Jesus Christ's promise that the "gates of Hades" would not prevail against his church.[*] In this case, quite literally, those gates—the temple of Pan—did not prevail against a church built in that very same spot!

[*] "Altar Dedicated to Pan Unearthed in Golan Heights" (December 2, 2020). Archaeology: A publication of the Archaeological Institute of America. Accessed on 19 October, 2023 at https://www.archaeology.org/news/9249-201202-golan-altar-pan

5
WHEN THE PRESSURE GETS TO YOU
MARK 14:26-72

NEW YORK
AUGUST 22, 1949

The New York Times carries a front page, banner headline: "BONES OF ST. PETER FOUND!" The cover of Time magazine also announces the discovery.

Someone has leaked the pope's secret.

Italian journalist Camille Gianfara (whose sources are still unknown) has the scoop of her career, the story of the secret excavations. The world clamors for confirmation from the Vatican, but the Holy See is silent. Over a year later, Pius XII breaks his silence during the international radio broadcast of Christmas Eve mass with a stunning announcement.

"Has Peter's tomb really been found?" he asks. "To this question, the answer is beyond all doubt, yes." But have his bones been found? "At the side of the tomb, human remains have been discovered," the pope says. "However, it is impossible to prove they belong to the body of the apostle."

He is careful with his public comments. But privately, he believes that Peter's bones have been found and rest in his apartment.

He is mistaken.

After several days of beautiful March weather in the Galilee region, I'm excited to finally follow Peter and Jesus to Jerusalem.

The big surprise: It's freezing.

I did not expect the rain, hail, and snow that greet me here. It is so bone-chillingly cold that when I explore the town, I have to wear every single shirt I packed for the trip to stay warm. Not kidding. Talk about standing out as a tourist: "Hello, I would like a coffee, and please pay no attention to the fact that I am wearing eight shirts."

Jerusalem is about a hundred-mile drive south of Capernaum and thousands of feet higher. My ears kept popping with each mile until I reached the city, set on steep hills 3,200 feet higher than the Sea of Galilee. That's why, in the Bible, people always talk about "going up" to Jerusalem, even if they're headed south. And that's why, as I discover, Jerusalem can be astonishingly cold. I've been there now twice during severe snowstorms and an ice storm. One day, I will learn my lesson and pack a winter coat.

All this explains a scene described by the gospel writers.

On another cold Jerusalem night, Simon Peter tries to warm himself around a courtyard fire. Also there, arms stretched toward the heat, are murderous enemies of Jesus. Standing shoulder to shoulder with them, Peter hopes he isn't recognized in the flickering light.

It's here at the fire that he has his most epic failure.

So you're part of a movement most of society thinks is pretty weird. Your friends don't share your values or your religion. There are constant temptations to excessive drinking and sexual immorality. You feel ostracized at times. There are times you compromise.

You're seriously thinking, "Maybe I am not just cut out for this Jesus stuff. Everyone else at church seems to have it together. I am so full of contradictions and flaws. Maybe I should quit."

I just described what it was like to be a Christian in the early Roman Empire. Sound familiar?

For some Christians, pressure turned into persecution. Many endured the cruel treatment Pliny the Younger later described to Emperor Trajan:

> "In the case of those who were denounced to me as Christians, I have observed the following procedure: I interrogated these as to whether they were Christians; those who confessed I interrogated a second and a third time, threatening them with punishment; those who persisted I ordered executed."[24]

They got three chances.

What would you do if the Roman governor called you into an arena, looked down from his judgment seat, and said, "We are only going to do this three times. Say, 'Caesar is Lord,' and you will live. Refuse, and you die. Number one ..."

Some Christians were willing to go to their death. But others gave in and denied Christ. Eventually, some of those nervously returned to church. There was considerable controversy over what to do with them. *Are they irredeemable traitors?*

I believe Peter told this story about himself to offer hope to those who had fallen—and to teach grace to those who hadn't.

Because he also had three chances. And failed each time.

Jesus and his friends have just finished the Last Supper. They are taking a late-night walk to an olive garden in Gethsemane where Jesus often liked to rest and pray. Along the way, he tells them, "All of you will desert me."

> Peter said to him, "Even if everyone else deserts you, I never will."
>
> Jesus replied, "I tell you the truth, Peter—this very night, before the rooster crows twice, you will deny three times that you even know me."
>
> "No!" Peter declared emphatically. "Even if I have to die with you, I will never deny you!" And all the others vowed the same. (Mark 14:29-31 NLT)

One of Peter's most consistent traits is his almost comedic level of overconfidence. Like here, when Peter looks around and rates himself morally better than all those other losers.

Overestimation of your own moral strength is a common trap. The truth is, given the right circumstances, I'm capable of any sin. And so are you. In fact, if you disagree with that statement, you're setting yourself up for a potential fall because of your overconfidence. (Example: "Even if all other weaklings pack a winter coat for Jerusalem, I can handle the cold and will only take a carry-on full of t-shirts.")

Suddenly there's a disturbance in the orchard. Torchlight. Clanging armor. The smell of sweat and fear. Judas leads a mob. They grab Jesus. Chaos erupts. Peter (of course!) waves his sword around and bravely injures... a servant. Not a soldier. Slicing off an... ear. Not a hand. Jesus sternly tells him to put that sword away before someone else gets hurt and heals the guy's head. Then he is led away. And the disciples flee.

Quiet returns to the garden.

But listen closely.

Peter and another unnamed disciple are hiding in the darkness of the grove.

Their hearts pound.

Their breath steams.

Their adrenalin pumps.

They watch as the light of torches winds back across the Kidron Valley into the walled city and they impulsively decide to follow, slithering from shadow to shadow, keeping a safe distance. They see Jesus led into the high priest's mansion. They hear the door slammed and bolted shut.

But they have one advantage. The man with Peter is known to the high priest. The guard at the gate recognizes him and lets both men in.

Archaeologists have unearthed impressive ruins of priestly homes from the time of Christ in Jerusalem. They are luxurious, split-level houses. One even includes a dungeon—an architectural feature prized by many clergy to this day. (Kidding.) (I hope.)

One recently discovered high priestly house had a vaulted ceiling, its own private bakery with three ovens, and a bathtub—an extremely rare luxury for the first century.[25]

These high priests were notoriously corrupt. Talmudic texts describe how the high priest sent out his gang to beat people up.[26] The Jewish writer Josephus notes, "But as for the high priest, Ananias ... he was a great hoarder up of money."[27]

I imagine the high priest Caiaphas patting himself dry, emerging freshly scrubbed from a long soak in his own tub. He greets these midnight conspirators in his fancy reception area, eager to silence this troublesome Jesus forever.

Peter has walked in with his friend and sees this all happening from a distance, through the doorway leading to the upper audience hall. He nervously edges toward the courtyard fire, shivering with cold and shock.

Even the fire is elite. It is a charcoal fire—more expensive than wood, but hotter and with less smoke, preferred by those with home fire pits. Peter tries to warm up there, desperately hoping he won't be recognized.

Those hopes are soon dashed.

Three Reasons I Fall

Peter will deny Jesus for the same three reasons I often fail to do the right thing:

1. I overestimate my strength.

While Jesus stands up to the pressure of his culture's most powerful figures in the next room, Peter is intimidated by a servant girl.

> One of the servant girls who worked for the high priest came by and noticed Peter warming himself at the fire. She looked at him closely and said, "You were one of those with Jesus of Nazareth." But Peter denied it. "I don't know what you're talking about," he said, and he went out into the entryway.
>
> Just then, a rooster crowed. (Mark 14:66-68 NLT)

I saw a lifeguard notice the other day that read: "You say you are a good swimmer, an experienced swimmer, a competitive swimmer. But you are no match for a rip current."

So I looked it up. Ocean rip currents can reach speeds of more than eight miles per hour. To put that in perspective, Olympic gold medalist swimmer Michael Phelps averaged five miles per hour. No human can outswim a strong rip current. Eighty percent of lifeguard rescues are related to them. Yet most people remain massively over-confident at the beach, certain they can handle it.

That's precisely Peter's problem.

2. I fear disapproval.

> When the servant girl saw him standing there, she began telling the others, "This man is definitely one of them!" But Peter denied it again. (Mark 14:69,70a NLT)

There is an epidemic right now of desperately seeking likes and fearing disapproval. We go along with the crowd, even when we think they might be wrong, to escape their judgment. You may feel Peter was weak, but let me ask, is there anyone whose opinion matters to you more than God's? People who comment on your social media posts? Co-workers? Friends? Those people have, in effect, become your god. You are letting their approval direct you. You will end up behaving in ways you could never defend. And like Peter, it can happen very quickly.

3. I act from insecurity, exhaustion, and fear.
Peter was feeling all three. When I'm tired, I turn into a different person. It's like I have a Jekyll and Hyde personality. That side of Peter is about to surface.

> A little later, some of the other bystanders confronted Peter and said, "You must be one of them because you are a Galilean." Peter swore, "A curse on me if I'm lying—I don't know this man you're talking about!" Immediately, the rooster crowed the second time. (Mark 14:71-72a NLT)

"I do not know him," is what he said, and on some level, I think he meant it. Peter had been expecting Jesus, this miracle worker with the power to stop storms and raise corpses, to humiliate these arrogant authorities. That's the Super-Messiah the disciples all expected. It was what Peter was hoping to see in that courtyard. Now Peter watches as Jesus behaves in a very un-Messiah-like way. Jesus is not using his power, or even his powerful words. Peter is crushed. He is confused. "I do not know this man." So he swears and curses.

This is even worse than it seems. The Greek word for "curse" does not just mean Peter said a bad word. It's the root of our English word "anathematize," which means to damn someone. The closest expression we have in English would be to combine the phrases "God damn you" and "go to hell." In Peter's culture, this was the very worst thing you could say to someone.

So who is Peter anathematizing? The original Greek translated as "a curse on me" actually doesn't have the words "on me." The literal Greek is, "he began to anathematize and to curse." Curse who? The object is unclear. He's either calling down this curse on himself: "May God damn me to hell if I am lying!" Which is bad because, uh, he is lying.

Or perhaps he's calling down this curse ... on Jesus. "You know what? To hell with that guy. God damn him. I don't care about him. I don't even know him. Leave me alone."

From the moment those words escaped his lips, Peter must have wondered whether he was indeed damned.

Three Keys to Recovery

We will all fail. That is not even in question. So the real question is, what do you do next? Woven into this story are three crucial means of recovery from a fall.

1. Grief.

Watch what happens immediately for Peter:

> Suddenly, Jesus' words flashed through Peter's mind:
> "Before the rooster crows twice, you will deny three times

that you even know me." And he broke down and wept.
(Mark 14:72a NLT)

He doesn't just weep. He *breaks*.

This is the beginning of his healing. One of my friends in our church recovery group put it this way: "To get past it, you have to go through it."

Grief is a healthy response. We're in a cultural moment where grief and lament are undervalued. We're desperate to always feel happy. Since failure feels terrible, we want to minimize the pain. Often, this means minimizing my failure, blaming my failure on someone else, or denying that I've failed altogether. But those responses short-circuit my recovery and only doom me to fail again.

As another pastor once told me, "You need to let godly sorrow do its work." Psalm 51 affirms, "The sacrifice God wants is a broken and contrite spirit." We can get so impatient to fix everything instantly that we don't allow healthy lament.

In recovery, they call this "hitting bottom." That's when you finally say, "God, I have been humbled by this. I don't think I can handle it anymore. Please, I need help."

Don't minimize the failure, don't justify the failure, and don't rationalize the failure. Own it. Admit it. Grieve it.

This moment of grief changed Peter.

Up to now, he thought following Jesus was all about his own strength: "Yes, Jesus, I have what it takes! I am a hero for God!" In this failure, he realizes, "It is not about my strength. It is not about my promises. It is not about my pledge of obedience. It is not about my force of will. It is about coming to God with empty hands, saying, 'I am weak. I have nothing. I throw myself on your grace.'"

How about you?
Is your internal monologue more typified by:

"I have what it takes."
"I won't blow it like others."
"I can power my way through." Or…

"I need you, Lord."
"I am a sinner in need of mercy."
"Help."
That's where you find healing.

2. Groups.

Let your friends support you. Let your small group support you. Let your family support you. Ask for help. Don't isolate.

Like Peter, three days later:

> (Mary Magdalene) went to the disciples, who were together grieving and weeping, and told them what had happened. (Mark 16:10)

Where are they? Together! What were they doing? Grieving, weeping. They shared their failure and loss in common. This is the power of 12-step groups. This is the power of small groups. This is the power of friendships.

But let me state the obvious: It's best to have a support system like this *before* a crisis occurs.

Sometimes people tell me, "I don't need to go to church. I can worship God by myself in the forest." I often answer, "That's right, you can. I hope you do! But a tree is not going to visit you in the hospital."

You need humans. So when you go through tough times, you go through them together.

3. Grace.

When the gospel writer Luke tells this story, he adds an intriguing comment from Jesus. Right after Peter insists he will never deny him, Jesus says,

> "Simon, Simon, Satan has asked to sift you all like wheat. But I have prayed for you, Simon, that your faith may not fail. So when you have repented and turned back to me, strengthen your brothers." (Luke 22:31-32)

Do you see grace all through that statement? Jesus makes a few things clear:

Jesus is never shocked when you fall.
He knew Peter would.
Jesus welcomes you back when you fall.
He tells Peter, when you have turned back, I will still have work for you.
Jesus prays for you when you fall.
Jesus prayed for Peter. Did you know Jesus prays for you, too?

The Bible says when we sin, he is our advocate before God the Father (1 John 2:1-2). He is sitting in the place of honor at God's right hand, pleading for us (Romans 8:34).

This image did not always comfort me.

The way I pictured it, Public Defender Jesus repeatedly goes to the Heavenly Father, who is sitting like a testy judge behind a massive bench. Jesus nervously clears his throat, "It's about René again, Father. Please give him one more chance." The Father replies, "Not again, he is a loser." Jesus pleads,

"Just for me? Give him another try." "OK. For you. But René is still a bozo."

In other words, Jesus acts like a defense attorney repping a repeat offender with no case, just pleading for mercy from the judge. And this made me nervous. Because I thought, "How long can he keep that up?"

Then I heard a sermon by one of my favorite pastors, Tim Keller. He said, "Would you please notice that it does not say Jesus is before the Father begging for mercy for you?" As he pointed out, 1 John 1:9 says God forgives us "because he is faithful *and just*." It is *just* for God to forgive us.

Jesus actually says something more like this: "Father, it's about René again. See that sin? I paid for it with my blood. Therefore, it is *just* that René not fall out of your favor. Ever. That sin doesn't need to be paid for twice. So I am asking for *justice*, because that sin is atoned for."

Jesus is not asking for leniency. Jesus is applying *justice* because that sin has been paid for—by him! He is not an advocate with a weak case. He is an advocate with an *infallible* case.

And that changes everything.

I once received this letter:

Dear Pastor René,

I am an inmate at the jail. I am one of those Christians who forgot that God loves me. Before I ended up in jail, I was literally drinking myself to death. I was on a path to Hell!

I lied to God and my family about my excessive drinking—even though it was quite apparent to everybody. I reached a point where all I wanted to do was crawl into a hole and die. I was—and felt—totally hopeless, alone, afraid, yet I could not stop drinking!

In a moment of clarity, I prayed something like this: "God, Father, forgive me of my sins, and please put someone or somebody in my life to guide me; your will, not mine be done."

Well, a few days later, I was promptly arrested by "God's taxi service," the Santa Cruz Police Department. At first, I was very angry, but as the days went by, I saw that God still loves me and was just disciplining me as a loving father.

I have rededicated my life and will to Jesus Christ. I am being honest for the first time in a long time. I do not know what God has in store for me, but this I do know:

I'm absolutely convinced that nothing, nothing living or dead, angelic or demonic, today or tomorrow, high or low, thinkable or unthinkable, absolutely nothing can get between us and God's love because of the way that Jesus, our master, has embraced us. Romans 8:38-39 (The Message)

Jesus was just waiting for his prayer.
You may have taken a giant step out of God's will.
You know when it was.

You know where it was.

You're thinking of it right now.

Whatever it is, whatever you have done, Jesus has been *praying for you*—for the moment you come home. The Bible says, "The Lord longs to be gracious to you" (Isaiah 30:18). He *longs* for you to receive his grace!

Let's circle back to an idea from the start of the chapter. The Gospel of Mark, said to be based on Peter's recollections, includes this very unflattering portrait of Peter.

Because Peter himself told this story.

Over and over again. It became his testimony. His brand. He wanted us to know what he discovered: Jesus makes amazing use of flawed followers.

> "We need not be defined by our failures. God does not define us by the very worst thing we ever did ... He continually invites us back, forgives us, restores us. Sometimes he uses us even more profoundly, not merely in spite of our flaws and failures but because of them. Jesus is the lord of the second chance. If the disciple who denied knowing Jesus became the Rock on which the church is built, there is hope for us too."—Adam Hamilton[28]

But how would Jesus help Peter get past this terrible shame?

Sometimes grace shows up best at breakfast.

WHEN THE PRESSURE GETS TO YOU

Watch a short video for this chapter filmed on location

DIGGING DEEPER:
WHERE DID CAIAPHAS INTERROGATE JESUS?

All four gospels describe Jesus' interrogation by the high priest. Two mention him by name: Caiaphas. Where in Jerusalem did this happen? Some traditions hold it was in a house now known as *Petrus in Gallicantu* (Latin for "Peter of the Rooster Crow").

I prefer another site. If you follow signs to a Jewish seminary, Yeshivat HaKotel, and take a small stairway down ten feet below its basement, you'll go back about 2,000 years to the most exclusive neighborhood in Jerusalem in Jesus' era.

Many experts believe this was Caiaphas' house (now part of the Wohl Museum)

After the Six-Day War in 1967, the Jewish Quarter was in ruins. This was a rare opportunity for archaeologists before the area was rebuilt. Here they found a wealthy residential neighborhood dating back to the days of Jesus. The most luxurious mansion covers 6,500 square feet and is designed like a Roman villa, with rooms around a central courtyard. A large reception hall has walls and floors lavishly decorated with colorful frescoes and mosaics. Archaeologists even found banquet platters, wine flasks, and ornate stone tables.

In the home next to this mansion, two inscriptions were found with the name "Kathros," the brother of Caiaphas (also a priest). It's not a stretch to imagine these two brothers living next door to each other.

The area is now known as the Wohl Museum. Could this be the estate of Caiaphas, complete with the courtyard where Peter denied Christ? The possibility is intriguing, though as yet there is no definitive proof.

6
WHEN YOU HAVE FALLEN
JOHN 21

ROME
MAY 1952

The presumed bones of Peter have been resting in Pope John XXIII's apartments for a decade.[29] The archaeological team is celebrated in journals as geniuses and pioneers.

Then the pope invites a non-Vatican employee to tour the excavation: Dr. Margherita Guarducci. A professor at the University of Rome, Guarducci is a world-renowned secular archaeologist with extensive field experience. She is also an expert epigraphist (the study of ancient writing), most famous for deciphering "The Gortyn Code," a mysterious language from 450 BC.

She is horrified at the damage the Vatican's inexperienced team inflicted on the tombs. She even discovers that puzzle pieces are missing; excavators have taken chunks of walls with ancient inscriptions to their homes!

Guarducci writes a scathing report and hands it to the pope. In response, he makes this educated critic his new head of excavations. The disgraced original team fumes and begins a smear campaign against Guarducci that lasts her entire life.

The pope decides to tap into more scientific expertise outside the Vatican. He invites one of Europe's most respected forensic anthropologists, Dr. Venerando Correnti, to examine the bones in his office and release a detailed report. After years of painstaking measurements and testing, Correnti reveals his findings.

These are not Peter's bones.

FLAWED FOLLOWER

They are from two men and one woman, plus several sheep, goats, horses, and cows. After analyzing and dating them, Dr. Correnti concludes none of the fragments belonged to Simon Peter.

But there are other bones that neither the pope nor Dr. Correnti know about.

I have escaped the chilly Jerusalem winter and find myself back on the warmer shores of the Sea of Galilee, at a spot called Tabgha, which means "Seven Springs," named for the warm springs that flow into the lake nearby.

There's a chapel here, the Church of St. Peter's Primacy, commemorating the events in John 21. I want to sneak behind the building, to a beach where fishermen have washed out their nets for centuries.

I sit on the rocky shore as early morning fishing boats glide past on the glassy water.

I close my eyes and imagine what Peter must have heard, felt, smelled, tasted.

Pebbles tumble in the waves, sounding like a hundred soft whispers.

Gulls cry.

I hear a boat motor. It's coming closer.

"Pastor René!" cries a husky voice. I open my eyes. "Oldest continuously operating boat on the lake!" yells Razi.

When you fail, it's not only that mistake that dogs you. It's the fear of *continued* failure.

You feel hopeless,
directionless,
uncertain,

anxious,

ashamed,

unworthy.

Your future prospects seem dismal.

You want to bench yourself.

This is the biggest temptation of failure. Freezing up. Staying stuck. Or even repeating the pattern because you don't think you deserve any better.

Maybe you're nodding in agreement right now, thinking,

"Yep. I relapsed—right after I publicly vowed I'd never do it again."

Or: "Lost my job. Lost my savings. Lost the trust of those I love. Lost my self-respect."

Or: "No one knows. But I fell and fell hard. Denied my principles. Now, the guilt haunts me. Along with a terrifying sense of unworthiness and total fear of discovery."

No matter the exact nature of your failure, you've probably thought: "Who am I to think I deserve anything good after failing so badly?"

As a pastor, I often see this in people who worry that their failure now defines them forever. Plus, I have felt this.

Eavesdrop on this next dialogue between Peter and Jesus. It's Christ's conversation with you, too.

When this happens, Peter has already seen the resurrected Jesus twice, in an upper room in Jerusalem. But if you read those accounts carefully, you'll notice something unusual. Peter hardly says a word (for once). Why?

Think about it. I imagine he felt stupid and ashamed. The last time he'd been with Jesus in that room, he'd boasted he would never deny him, even if all the others did. Then he fell flat on his face. Denied Jesus three times. Now Jesus is back? Peter likely thought, "Yeah, to fire me. I was unfaithful, unreliable. He is going to dismiss me. Or even damn me."

On the day of the resurrection, an angel addresses several women at the empty tomb of Jesus. They are to tell the other disciples Jesus is alive. Hear what he tells them carefully:

> "But go, tell his disciples and Peter, 'He is going ahead of you into Galilee. There you will see him, just as he told you.'"
> (Mark 16:7)

His disciples ... *and Peter*. Every other time Peter is mentioned in the gospels in a list, his name comes first. This time, he is dead *last*.

Peter knew he had an appointment with Jesus in Galilee. But Peter is not expecting a helpful job evaluation. He is expecting to get fired. So he goes. He will accept responsibility. He will leave the fold. It's what he deserves.

> Simon Peter said, "I'm going fishing." "We'll come, too," they all said. So they went out in the boat, but they caught nothing all night. (John 21:3)

Peter is saying, in so many words, "I quit." He figures he's disqualified anyway, so he goes back to his old job. Drags six other disciples along with him. They're night fishing, which is fine with him. The dark of the night matches his mood.

Then Peter's a failure even at that. The sun rises, their nets are empty, and some early-bird hiker yells from shore, "Catch anything, boys?" I see Peter a little irritated, shouting back, *"No!"*

Then that figure they can't quite make out in the dim light says, "Try the other side of the boat!"

Well. That brings back an interesting memory.

Three years before, Jesus had told an exhausted Simon, who had nothing to show for a hard night of fishing, to cast his nets one more time—and his crew bagged out, caught so much their gear broke. So when Peter and the others hear this suggestion from the man on shore, they look at each other, shrug, flip the net to the other side—and instantly, their boat is nearly capsized by hundreds of fish rushing in.

"It's the Lord!" says one and of course Peter, ever impulsive, cannonballs into the waves and swims to shore.

What happens next is astonishing. But you need to smell it to believe it.

"When they landed, they saw a fire of burning coals there with fish on it, and some bread." (John 21:9)

Jesus is serving breakfast. Today's specials: Toast. Fried fish. And grace.

These guys had abandoned Jesus, denied him, doubted him. Only the women had stayed with Christ. When Jesus gets these men together, back on home ground, away from the Jerusalem crowds, what does he do?

No stern sermon. No long lecture. No condemning gaze. Just, "Who's hungry?"

You blow it. Jesus finds you. You cringe, waiting for what's next. And he says, "You look tired. Have a seat, enjoy the sunrise, eat some bread—just baked it myself!"

That's grace.

There's an easily overlooked detail in verse nine: Jesus made a fire out of *coals*. Intriguing. Why specify that?

The Greek word *anthrakia* (from which we get our English word "anthracite," meaning a charcoal fire) is found only twice in the New Testament. The second time is here. The first time is in John 18:18, where it's the word used for the courtyard fire *where Peter denied Jesus.*

Jesus doesn't just gather wood for this fire. He makes the effort to bring in charcoal.

You know how smells bring back memories?

For me?
Popcorn = movie matinees.
Aftershave = my dad.
Coffee = morning.
Campfires = fun.
For Peter, charcoal fires = the worst failure of his life.

Last time Peter had been near an *anthrakia*, he had spoken the *anathema*.

Jesus builds this fire as if to say, "Hey Peter. Smell that? You were asked three questions around a fire like this. Let's try that again. Let's rebrand that experience." He takes the trigger for Peter's trauma and turns it around.

With three questions of his own.

"When they had finished eating, Jesus said to Simon Peter,
'Simon son of John, do you love me more than these?'"
(John 21:15)

Jesus asks not,
"Do you promise never to do that again?"
"Do you feel ashamed of yourself?"
"Will you try harder next time?"
Jesus asks,
"Do you love me?" Times three.

That voice inside your head, the one that whispers, "How can you call yourself a Christian? How could you do that? Why don't you just give up?" That is not the voice of Jesus.

Think of what this tells us about discipleship. At the end of his time with Simon Peter, after three years of walking together, Christ's question to him is not, "So *now* do you finally understand? Are all your answers right on the test at last? Are you firmly committed this time?"

It's, "Do you *love* me?"

Following Jesus does not necessarily lead to all the answers about Jesus. Following Jesus does not lead to perfection in this life (though it does lead to growth). **Following Jesus leads to loving Jesus.** Then overflowing with that love toward others.

Three times Jesus asks.

Three times Peter answers.

Verse 15: "Yes, Lord," he answered, "You know I love You."

Verse 16: "Yes, Lord," he answered, "You know I love You."

Verse 17: "Lord, You know all things," he replied. "You know I love You."

Here's where it gets a little nerdy, but hang with me. There's a payoff.

In Greek, Peter uses a different word for love than Jesus: The first two times Jesus asks, "Do you love me?" Jesus uses *agape*, the word for perfect, ideal, unconditional, divine love. But when Peter responds, "You know I love you," he uses *phileo*, the word for brotherly love.

It's like Peter is suggesting, "Well, though my love for you is not what it *should* be, I do love you on at least *this* level." He could not dare claim *agape*, but he could offer *phileo*.

For Peter, that's progress! Up to this point, Peter has been overestimating himself—a lot. Every time Jesus tells the truth about himself or about his disciples—"You will all deny me," for example—Peter interrupts by turning his own performance predictions up: "They may all ditch you, but not me." Then up another notch: "In fact, I will die with you!"

Here he turns it *down* a notch. The old Peter might have added, "Yes indeed, I love you with the highest love—more than these other fools!" Instead, he is humbled: "Well, I can tell you I love you like a brother."

Then Jesus switches to Peter's word for love, *phileo*, in his final question. "Do you? Do you, Peter, do you *phileo* me?"

John writes that Peter was hurt, possibly because Jesus had a point. Peter's actions didn't support brotherly love either. What kind of brother runs away like he did?

It's compelling that in Peter's third reply, he doesn't just say, "You know I love you." He says, "Lord, you know everything." *Everything*.

You know how much I fail you.
You know how imperfectly I follow you.
Yet you also know I *do* still love you.

And that is enough for Jesus.

Jesus does not want outrageous pledges of loyalty or performative attempts to prove our worth. Peter was full of all that, and look where it got him. Jesus wants our love. Because that is the fuel for true growth.

Even our inconsistent, well-meaning, clumsy, mixed-up attempts at following Jesus are accepted by him. It's not that Jesus wants us to stay there. It's that Jesus knows we *will* mature—if we keep following.

Then Jesus replies, three times.

Verse 15: "Feed my lambs."
Verse 16: "Take care of my sheep."
Verse 17: "Feed my sheep."

Jesus is not looking for yet another dramatic declaration from Peter. He is connecting Peter's love to *action*—to care for his people.

Discipleship is not in the dramatic. Discipleship is in the daily.

If you've fallen like Peter, your love for Jesus is demonstrated not by emotional "recommitment" pledges never to fall again or by feats of fanatical devotion that you imagine show your true zeal. That's your inner Simon talking.

Your devotion to Jesus is shown by your devotion to the people Jesus loves.

Feed my sheep.

That might mean giving someone a ride.

Meeting someone's need for food or clothing or shelter.

Visiting them when they are sick or in prison.

Praying or studying the Bible with them.

Or simply being their friend and listening.

Jesus asks three times. Peter answers three times. Jesus restores him three times.

Once for every single time Peter denied him.

This beautiful early morning beach dialogue between them was meant to be overheard. By the other disciples, sure. But also by John's readers.

The author of the Gospel of John, writing late in the first century, knew there were thousands of Christians struggling with guilt. Like Peter, they had once chosen to follow Jesus with sincere devotion. But many had denied Jesus in the face of Caesar's representatives, from whom they had heard the three dreaded questions.

They needed to know that Jesus was asking them three questions too.

Do you love me?

"But I failed."

Do you love me?

"But I crumbled."

Do you love me?

"But I publicly denied you."

For them, like for Peter, Jesus was still standing there, still calling, still inviting.

Follow me.

How many times does Jesus invite you back?

Once for every single time you fall.

I don't want to leave this point yet. Because I don't think you believe it.

The assignment Jesus gave Peter was not some demotion. It was his plan for Peter from the start.

It can be easy to assume God must be so disappointed with you that he will withhold his blessing. You choked in your last at-bat so badly that you're cut from the team. You blew Plan A, so now you are on the lesser Plan B—or C or D or Z.

But Jesus doesn't punish you with Plan B. *He rewrites Plan A.*

Of course, Jesus' grace toward you is not an endorsement of your immaturity.

His grace is an embrace.

It's a call to come home.

It's a warm breakfast on a cold morning after a sleepless, unproductive night.

Have you failed?

Smell the toast and feel the fire's warmth and hear his gentle voice.

Follow me. Have some breakfast.

But Jesus has something else to say to Peter. It sounds grim, but really it's a gift.

"*Truly, truly, I tell you,*" he says. That's Jesus for, "Listen up."

> "Truly, truly, I tell you, when you were young, you dressed yourself and walked where you wanted; but when you are old, you will stretch out your hands, and someone else

will dress you and lead you where you do not want to go."
(John 21:18)

"You will stretch out your hands …" is a euphemism for crucifixion. Jesus is telling Peter, "When you get old, you're going to be crucified—like me."

Though the details of Peter's death are not in the Bible, some of the oldest stories Christians ever told each other were about Peter's death in Rome under Nero. He was given an opportunity to deny Jesus and be set free. But he wouldn't do it. So he was crucified.

Why would Jesus hint at Peter's gruesome end? Read the next verse:

> Jesus said this to indicate the kind of death by which Peter would glorify God. (John 21:19a)

Not just what *kind* of death.
How he would *glorify God* through his death.
Jesus is saying, in effect, "Peter, I want to tell you something. I know you said you would not deny me. It didn't work out that way last time. *It will next time.*"

Jesus was telling Peter that he saw remarkable growth in his future. Peter would become more and more like a Rock. He was not doomed to an endless loop of failure. In his final moment of truth, he would stay faithful.

Jesus says the same to you. The promise is in Scripture many times:

> I am certain that God, who began the good work within you, will continue his work until it is finally finished on the day when Christ Jesus returns. (Philippians 1:6)

Do not give up. God is faithful. He is working in you. All is not lost.

You will get unstuck.

You will move forward.

Jesus will complete the process he started in you.

Even your failures will become part of your redemption history.

> "God uses broken things. It takes broken soil to produce a crop, broken clouds to produce rain, broken grain to give bread, broken bread to give strength. It is the broken alabaster box that gives forth perfume ... and it is Peter, weeping bitterly, who returns to greater power than ever."
>
> - Vance Havner[30]

Question: Why didn't Jesus just reinstate Peter back in Jerusalem? Why did he wait to meet them in Galilee? Why the change of scenery?

I think he was communicating, *Look, Peter, I called you out of being a fisherman right at this very shore three years ago, and now—knowing everything I know about you—I would do it again.*

I chose you then.

I choose you still.

And I will never un-choose you.

Jesus chose you. And Jesus will never un-choose you. Aren't you glad?

(And listen. I feel like I shouldn't have to restate the obvious, but just because Jesus forgives you doesn't mean you should keep on deliberately blowing it because you've got this safety net. Jesus will forgive you no matter how many times you hit yourself in the face with a hammer, but there are a lot of other excellent reasons to stop hitting yourself in the face with a hammer.)

Then Jesus said to him, "Follow me!" (John 21:19b)

Did you catch the symmetry? Jesus' last words to Peter in the gospels are the same as his first: *Follow me.*

The way I picture the scene, Jesus turns and starts walking away. Peter takes a couple steps to follow—perfect time for a slow fade to black. Jesus just delivered the ideal tag line. I hear the orchestral film score swelling. Long drone shot of the sunrise over Galilee as our camera pulls away from Jesus and Peter strolling on the sand. Credits roll. Fade to black.

Needle scratch. Hold everything. Peter has to ruin it by talking too much. Again! This man does not know how to read the moment.

Peter turns around and sees "the disciple Jesus loved," who isn't named, but most scholars believe was John.

When Peter saw him, he asked, "Lord, what about him?"
(John 21:21)

Like: "Uh, I appreciate what you said about how I'd be crucified, and how I would glorify God in my grisly death, thank you for that, super encouraging, but what about him?

You always liked him best. You gonna let him be crucified and glorify you too?"

> Jesus answered, "If I want him to remain alive until I return, what is that to you? You must follow me."
> (John 21:22)

We were meant to overhear that part of the conversation too.

Don't compare yourself with somebody else.

Don't worry about how Jesus deals with anybody else.

Don't think you are being treated worse by God than anyone else.

You follow Jesus wherever that leads. *For you.* What God intends for others is irrelevant to the question: Will *you* follow Jesus?

Jesus had a different plan for John. He lived outside the public eye for many years, quietly taking care of Jesus' mother Mary as she grew old.

Incidentally, ancient sources say that during the reign of the Roman Emperor Domitian, John was tossed into a cauldron of boiling oil. Didn't kill him though. He was later sent into exile on a prison island. So "the disciple Jesus loved" didn't exactly get off easy.

Here's the point. **Comparison is a trap.**

As Rick Warren wrote,

> "There are two reasons you should never compare yourself with anyone else. First, you will always be able to find someone who seems to be doing a better job than you and become discouraged. Or you will find someone who doesn't seem as effective as you, and you will get full of pride ...

We are all on the same team; we have been given different assignments; we are all uniquely shaped."[31]

You know what astonishes me? Here's the risen Jesus, with resurrection-level, walking-through-walls, ascending-into-clouds, appearing-and-disappearing power. He could have done anything, gone anywhere. But what he chooses to do with all that power is find one guy. And restore him.

Because that's how Jesus *always* uses power. He came to find the lost sheep. Like Peter. And like you.

Pastor Ray Johnston retells the story of a Chicago-area pastor's first Little League baseball game:

I'm the youngest guy on the team. I'm the least skilled on the team. I'm the skinniest guy on the team.

I played right field. Even when you're only eight, you know why you're in right field. You're there because never in the recorded history of Little League has a ball ever been hit to right field.

I came up to bat three times and struck out every time.

Then it was the seventh and last inning, the bases were loaded, and our team was behind by one run. I was up ... and the second I looked at the pitcher's mound, I knew I had no shot. The pitcher stood at least six feet, nine inches tall and sported a full beard— at least, that's how a ten-year-old looked to an eight-year-old.

FLAWED FOLLOWER

He wound up. I didn't even see his first pitch. Whoosh! I heard the umpire yell, "Strike one!" The pitcher wound up and threw his second pitch—Whoosh! "Strike two!"

And then I made a mistake—I looked around. I saw two hundred people on their side, standing up and screaming for me to strike out and lose the game. On the other side, I saw two hundred people, including sixty of my relatives, standing up and screaming for me to get a hit and win the game. Shaking, I stepped back into the box, and said to myself, "I gotta get a hit." So for the first time ever, I swung. I swung as hard as I could.

And ...

I ...

Missed ...

I heard the ball hit the catcher's mitt, and the umpire say, "Strike three, you're out! Game over." Huge cheer erupted from two hundred people, an audible groan from two hundred other people—and I knew I had failed.

I dropped the bat at home plate and started the longest walk of my life, up the first base line to the dugout. I sat down, pulled my hat over my eyes, and sobbed. It was the last game of the day, and I could hear the gravel scrunch underneath car tires as people pulled out of the parking lot. Everything got quiet.

Then, I heard a noise from the pitcher's mound. A voice said, "Hey, son, get back up. The game ain't over."

There, on the pitcher's mound, stood my dad. I looked and saw that none of my relatives had left. They were all in the field, waiting to play.

I sheepishly walked over to the plate. My dad threw a pitch, and everybody started cheering. I missed.

He threw it again. I missed again.

About fifteen pitches later, my dad threw it right down the middle and whack! I knocked it into left field. I stood at home plate, and my dad said, "What are you doing? Run!"

Okay, where's first base? I'd never been there. I ran down to first base, just in time to see Aunt Emma throw the ball into center field. I thought, Cool, I'm going to get a double! I ran to second base, just in time to see my cousin Todd, a pretty good athlete playing center field, throw the ball into right field where my nearly blind Uncle Joe was standing. As I ran to third base, all I knew was, they've thrown the ball to a blind guy and I'm gonna score!

I rounded third and sprinted toward home. When I got about ten feet away, I dove for the plate, slid across, jumped up.

And then I saw him. About five feet in front of me was my dad. He'd gotten down on one knee. Tears were streaming down his face. He held out his arms and said, "Son, welcome home. You're safe." I threw myself into his arms. He picked me up and whispered, "I told you the game wasn't over."

My relatives ran onto the infield and carried me off the field cheering as the sun set on the little baseball field in Nowhere, Iowa.[32]

Jesus is saying to Peter—and to you—"The game's not over. Get off the bench."

Failure is inevitable. You're human. But if you're willing to learn and grow—and keep following Jesus—it doesn't have to have the last word.

Peter is back in the game. But he could never have imagined the controversy he was about to ignite.

Watch a short video for this chapter filmed on location

DIGGING DEEPER
PETER'S LATER YEARS

Although the Bible does not include much detail about Peter's later years, several works by early Christian authors offer tantalizing glimpses. Whether these stories are legends or history is impossible to say, but they certainly preserve how Peter was remembered by the earliest believers.

Clement of Rome, who lived from around AD 35 to AD 99, apparently knew both Peter and Paul personally and wrote about their martyrdoms in Rome (*First Clement 5:1-4*). The Acts of Peter, written about a century later, describes how Peter was condemned to be crucified in Rome. He then makes a strange request: To be crucified upside down.

The philosopher Titus Flavius Clemens, also known as Clement of Alexandria, was a convert to Christianity born in AD 150. He records several traditions he had heard about Peter; for example, Peter's wife traveled with him on his missionary journeys, not only as his marriage partner but also as his missionary helper. According to Clement, Peter's wife was arrested and executed first, and "the blessed Peter, when he beheld his wife on her way to execution ... addressed her by name and with words of exhortation and good cheer, bidding her to remember the Lord ... such was the marriage of those blessed ones."*

Clement of Alexandria also passes along a tradition about Peter's daughter (a story found in several ancient sources): When she was ten years old, she became paralyzed on one side of her body and was never healed.

* Clement of Alexandria, *Strom.* 7.63.3

7
WHEN SURPRISING DOORS OPEN
ACTS 10

ROME
1953

Dr. Margherita Guarducci retrieves a large chunk of the shrine wall from the home of the ousted director of excavations. She realizes that the Greek letters on the fragment align perfectly with other letters already on the wall.

To her astonishment, when this missing puzzle piece is fitted into the wall, the complete sentence reads, in Greek, "Peter is buried in here."

Intrigued, Guarducci descends into the underground tombs every morning for five years, meticulously photographing other ancient inscriptions on the wall next to Peter's shrine. Every afternoon, she pores over the evidence. No one had ever seriously studied these puzzling scratches and inscriptions; they had been ignored in a headlong search for bones. Guarducci finds Peter's name more than twenty times plus numerous Christian symbols associated with Peter and Jesus.[33]

One morning Guarducci descends into the tombs and finds Giovanni Segoni, foreman of the Vatican facility team, stringing work lights. Striking up a casual conversation, she asks if he knows about any interesting finds she might have missed.

"Yes," he answers. "There are bones."

Not the ones taken by the pope to his apartments. Other bones.

Segoni then tells her a story she has never heard, the story of the old priest who carefully boxed and recorded the bones strewn around by the previous team. Segoni was the young worker who came into the tombs with the priest nightly.

He tells her that one night, they found a small marble-lined enclosure inside the wall of the ancient shrine. Inside the marble box were bones, which seemed to be wrapped in fine cloth.

Fearing the archaeologists would dishonor them, Segoni and the priest carefully placed these bones into a wooden box, labeled them, and took them to a locked storage room in the basement of St. Peter's, where they still rested on a shelf.

He knows exactly where the box is. Would Dr. Guarducci like to see it?

THE MEDITERRANEAN COAST
PRESENT DAY

It's a warm spring night in the ancient port of Joppa, or Jaffa as it is known today. And I am lost.

Jaffa is soaked in Mediterranean atmosphere. There is a luxury hotel built out of a Crusader castle. Stone minarets peer above old buildings like little lighthouses. Trendy cafes, galleries, and boutiques line narrow streets. Earlier in the day I enjoyed shakshuka (eggs baked in tomato sauce) with my wife at a café near the famous flea market.

It's a pleasant place to be lost. But still. I'm lost.

The alleys converge at odd angles, and I keep finding myself back at the same little stand where kids are selling oranges until finally I give in and buy one so I can ask directions without feeling impolite. How do I get to the harbor? Ah, of course. Just follow the slope down.

I follow twisty, narrow paths paved with white limestone blocks fluorescent under the full moon. When I reach the port, it's like a movie set from Casablanca: Street lamps cast a saffron glow over the bobbing skiffs tied to the piers. Jaffa is the oldest working seaport on the planet, and it certainly has an ancient patina. As I capture some photos, I try to imagine the characters that cruised into this harbor over its 38 centuries of operation.

Solomon used it. Jonah fled through it. Richard the Lionheart sailed into it. Napoleon conquered it. Razi fished in it. Just kidding about Razi.

And starting in Jaffa, something happened that changed the course of history.

Peter opened a door.

In Acts chapter 10, Peter is staying here at the house of Simon the Tanner (there's still a house that claims to be the actual place). He's getting hungry for lunch. As the meal is prepped, he goes up on the roof to pray.

Then he has a vision. He sees something like a picnic blanket let down from heaven with all kinds of food in it. So far, that might not seem a surprising dream for a hungry guy.

But this picnic is puzzling.

It contains non-kosher food jumbled together with kosher food. He hears a voice telling him to get up and eat whatever he wants.

Peter is perplexed.

Religiously observant Jews don't eat non-kosher food, such as shellfish, pork, rabbits, or fish without scales (like eels). There are also dozens of non-kosher bird species, and all reptiles are forbidden. Yet Peter sees "all kinds" of four-footed animals, reptiles, and birds in this vision of lunch.

He apparently thinks this is a test. Get up and eat *this* stuff? "Of course not, Lord!" he objects.

Then he hears these words:

"Do not call anything impure that God has made clean."
(Acts 10:15)

This happens three times.

Peter's still trying to work out what it means—when suddenly, there's a knock on the door.

Anyone would be rattled to see who is there: Representatives of Rome. Their commander has sent them to escort Peter about 34 miles north along the coast to Caesarea Maritime, a gleaming new city covered in marble and gold, built from the ground up to look and feel like Rome. It was an imperial colony right there in Judea.

Begun by Herod and finished by Hadrian, this aqueduct brought water to Caesarea from hills 10 miles away.

One of the most technologically advanced cities of its day, Caesarea was built as a spectacular beachside resort by Herod the Great around 10 BC to honor the Roman emperor. Since there was no harbor between the ancient ports of Jaffa and Dor—a 40-mile stretch—Herod created one. It was the largest artificial harbor in the world at the time, as large as the port of Athens, built with history's first use of hydraulic concrete.

The city boasted two massive theaters, two racetracks, two huge pagan temples for the worship of Caesar and of Rome, a jaw-dropping seaside palace, and the regional headquarters of the Roman army and government.

Most of these buildings were thought to be lost forever. But starting in the late 1950s and continuing until today, large-scale archaeological digs have unearthed most of these legendary structures, which had been buried in sand for centuries. I have taught groups on the steps of the ancient theater here.

In 1961, archaeologists unearthed part of a temple dedicated to Emperor Tiberius. The chief donor's name was carved into the stone: Roman prefect Pontius Pilate – the man who signed Jesus' death warrant.

For Peter, this is precisely the wrong direction. He had only recently experienced a miraculous prison escape. The Roman puppet king, Herod Agrippa, had wanted to kill him. Now these agents of Rome are asking him to please accompany us, sir, right back into the lion's den. I might have jumped across the alley to the next roof and run for my life. Peter invites them in for lunch. The following day, they walk north to that new Roman colony.

And it's there Peter meets a man unlike him in every way imaginable.

> In Caesarea there lived a Roman army officer named
> Cornelius, who was a captain of the Italian regiment.
> (Acts 10:1)

> Cornelius is not just a Gentile; he is a Roman.
> He is not just a Roman; he is a soldier.
> He is not just a soldier; he is a commander.

He is not just a commander; he commands the *Italian* regiment.

You could not create a more non-Jewish person in a laboratory.

Yet something was happening with the Gentiles all over the Empire. Many were dissatisfied with the pagan gods. They had begun worshipping the one universal God as best they understood him. The God of the Bible was appealing. But there were many roadblocks, not the least of which was male circumcision. Plus Gentiles were not allowed past strict barriers erected at the Temple. That meant many Romans and Greeks stood on the outside looking in. Literally. That was Cornelius. Longing for God but pushed away by religion.

One day, he also has a vision: To send for Peter. The Holy Spirit was already at work in this centurion's soul, long before Peter had ever said a word to him.

When Peter arrives, Cornelius falls at his feet to worship him.

> But Peter made him get up. "Stand up," he said, "I am only a man myself." (Acts 10:26)

Then Peter makes a history-altering choice. His next step may have been even scarier for him than walking onto the surface of the lake that stormy night long ago. He walks across a Roman threshold. Into the house.

> He said to them, "You know how unlawful it is for a Jew to associate with a foreigner or visit him. But God has shown me that I should not call any man impure or unclean." (Acts 10:28)

In the Judaism of Peter's day, even the homes of Gentiles were considered non-kosher. Forbidden. Taboo. Yet Peter has connected the dots. He's quoting that vision from the day before. But he now realizes those words were not just about food. They were about *people*.

"Do not call anything impure that God has made clean."

Imagine what a stretch this was for Peter.

He'd once assumed Jesus was a military Messiah on a mission to ruin Romans. Now he's welcoming Romans—Roman soldiers!—into the Jesus family.

Think of all the ways this was uncomfortable for him: Peter was a rural blue-collar fisherman with zero experience navigating Roman culture. Now he is in a beautiful Roman home facing Roman soldiers. Images of Roman gods populate the floor mosaics and wall frescoes. He can barely make out the Latin they're all speaking. The pork smells delicious.

Now imagine what a stretch this was for *Cornelius*.

Let's start with his name. "Cornelius" was a family name used by people from the *gens*, or house, of Cornelia, one of the greatest patrician houses of ancient Rome. For over seven hundred years, the House Cornelia produced more politicians and generals than any other Roman family. These were the Kennedys and Roosevelts of Rome. Cornelius was likely from this family. Then there's his job. Roman officers were professional men with specialist skills in literacy and accountancy.

So Cornelius was from an elite family, with an elite education and an elite position, in an elite new royal city.

Cornelius was Ivy League.

Peter was Duck Dynasty.

What did these two have in common?

Only Jesus.

Who do you hate?

Maybe hate is too strong a word, but is there a group you despise? Judge? Exclude?

Maybe that Jew-Gentile divide is not what's troubling you. But if you're honest with yourself, there's some other divide.

You wear flip-flops and shorts and judge those uptight people in suits and ties.

You drive a Prius and eat vegan and are secretly sure you must be better morally than your SUV-driving, BBQ-eating neighbors.

You're a progressive tree-hugger who can hardly imagine being friends with the cowboy conservatives you see when you venture to their (red)neck of the woods.

Or reverse any of those sentences.

And it gets more complicated.

What about those women from the drug treatment center who attend church each week as part of their program? *Can't someone please tell them to dress a little more ... appropriately?*

What about those teenagers over there smoking? *I wouldn't want my kids in youth group with the likes of them.*

Or maybe you're a woman in the program, or one of those teens. *Those church people are so judgy. What a bunch of uptight hypocrites.*

Everybody calm down. Hear the voice from the vision:

"Do not call anything impure that God has made clean."

Give people time to grow. Direct them toward the grace of God that will change them from the inside out.

That's what Peter does next.

Cornelius explains his vision, and Peter replies

> "I now realize how true it is that God does not show favoritism but accepts from every nation the one who fears him and does what is right." (Acts 10:34,35)

Radical statement. Massive development in the Jesus movement. Peter realizes the extent of the kingdom. Every race. Every nation. Every class. Divine diversity. No one had ever preached anything like this before, not in any religion on earth.

Pay close attention to what Peter tells Cornelius about Jesus:

> "We are witnesses of everything he did ..." (Acts 10:39a)

Everything he did.

Just think about what Peter had witnessed.

He could have told Cornelius how Jesus healed his mother-in-law.

He could have shared how Jesus helped him walk on water.

He could have described the waves flattening.

The nets filling.

Jesus shining.

But what he chooses to tell him is this:

They killed him by hanging him on a cross, but God raised him from the dead on the third day and caused him to be seen. (Acts 10:39b-40)

Of all his amazing experiences, this is the one Peter treasures most. This is the one that changed his life. This is the story he can't stop retelling.

I like the example Peter is setting.

We all love hearing dramatic stories of changed lives. Not many of you know how I was saved: After being kicked out of the military for going AWOL to seek treasure in Iraq, I was recruited by the Swiss mafia. I quickly became a well-connected dealer in stolen antiquities, accumulating yachts and mansions, but they left me feeling empty. Finally, on a solo spiritual quest while climbing Mount Everest, I had a vision of Jesus calling me to repent.

None of that is true. Sometimes I wish it was! I can feel my story is boring. The truth: Despite our early tragedies, My mom loved me. I grew up enjoying church. I found Jesus as my Savior when I was a kid. Not that exciting.

Peter lived a much more exciting life than I, but what he loved to share was this: The risen Jesus saved him. He would tell you that's the most exciting part of your story too. Whenever Peter teaches anyone in the Book of Acts, he always starts with this: Jesus died and rose again so that all who trust in Him can find life. Death and sin are the real enemies the Messiah came to vanquish.

> "All the prophets testify about him that everyone who believes in him receives forgiveness of sins through his name." (Acts 10:43)

Peter offers the invitation he first heard on a lakeshore to these seekers on a seashore.

Follow Jesus.

Before Cornelius can even say the "yes" bubbling up in his heart, the Holy Spirit falls upon them all. Peter says, "Surely no one can stand in the way of their being baptized with water. They have received the Holy Spirit just as we have."

Just as we have.

Just as Peter and his friends were called, Cornelius and friends have been called. Just as Peter and his friends received the Holy Spirit at Pentecost, now Cornelius and his household have too.

Peter is growing. His old views are changing.

He was called, he learned, he grew, he fell, he was restored—and he is now calling others to Christ.

He has become a fisher of men.

Peter takes the keys Jesus gave him and unlocks a massive door.

Peter realizes the gospel is not a Judean gospel. It is not a Roman gospel. It is not a Greek gospel or an African gospel or an Arab gospel. The gospel is not an American gospel. The gospel is not a European gospel. It is not a gospel of the rich or the poor or the black or the white or the Democrats or the Republicans. It welcomes them all while transcending them all to create one new family out of them all.

Jesus came to include everyone.

This means you.

Maybe other doors have been locked or slammed in your face. Now a door opens. On the other side is Jesus. Inviting you in.

Of course, this doesn't mean he validates all our opinions or behaviors. As N.T. Wright puts it,

"It means there are no ethnic or geographical or cultural or moral barriers any longer in the way of anyone and everyone being offered forgiveness and new life. That is a message far more powerful than the easygoing laissez-faire tolerance which Western society so easily embraces. Cornelius didn't want God to tolerate him. He wanted to be welcomed, forgiven, healed, transformed. And he was."[34]

Cornelius was as far from Jesus as anyone. But when he sought the truth, Jesus found him.

If you're sincerely seeking after God, he'll make sure you're found. That's a promise. Jesus said, "If you seek, you will find." (Matthew 7:7)

Cornelius and his friends rejoice in their new faith! They're baptized! High-fives all around!

But all is not sunshine and fish sauce.

Because the next week at church, there's an influx of clean-shaven, Latin-speaking, shrimp-breath Romans sitting next to bearded, orthodox Jewish Jesus followers. Super awkward.

The anti-Gentile emotions in Judea were running high. First-century Jewish writer Josephus described how intense it got:

"Eleazar, the son of Ananias, the high priest, who was at that time governor of the Temple, persuaded those that officiated to receive no gift or sacrifice for any foreigner. And this was the true beginning of our war with the Romans, for the priests rejected even the sacrifice of Caesar on this account ..."[35]

Did you catch that?

The religious establishment in Jerusalem was pushing Gentiles out—even Caesar.

Simon Peter was welcoming Gentiles in—even centurions.

Christians were affected by their culture then, just as we are now. The heightened tension between Gentile and Jew infected the church, and two camps quickly developed. The new outsiders were so repulsive to many insiders, so unclean, so unholy, that their conversions were not trusted. The old-school, old-guard religionists wanted a long intense process to sift the committed from the pretenders.

The agitation intensifies until a meeting is called in Jerusalem. Many stand up to angrily insist the Gentiles first must convert to Judaism even to be considered Christians.

Peter opened this door. They're trying to slam it shut.

Finally, Peter asks to speak. He is fired up.

> "Why do you try to test God by putting on the necks of Gentiles a yoke that neither we nor our ancestors have been able to bear?" (Acts 15:10)

A heavy yoke. A burden. The law of Moses was good. But some leaders had turned it into a performative religion. It had become unbearable. Peter says,

> "No! We believe it is through the grace of our Lord Jesus that we are saved, just as they are." (Acts 15:11)

He insists there is only one way anyone can possibly be saved. Or ever was saved.

It's the word at the core of our faith.

Grace.

Grace means it's all a gift. Your salvation is all God. Imagined by God. Initiated by God. Finished by God. Given by God.

Paul and James back Peter up, and the decision is made: Gentiles are allowed in.

And in they still come. Drawn by grace.

Irish singer Bono, leader of the famous band U2, was drawn in. In an interview with journalist Michka Assayas, he said:

> "The thing that keeps me on my knees is the difference between grace and karma. At the center of all religions is the idea of karma. You know, what you put out comes back to you ... reaping what is sown. And yet, along comes this idea called grace to upend all that ... which in my case is very good news indeed, because I've done a lot of stupid stuff. I'd be in big trouble if karma were going to finally be my judge. It doesn't excuse my mistakes, but I'm holding out for grace. I'm holding out that Jesus took my sins onto the cross, because I know who I am, and I hope I don't have to depend on my own religiosity."

At this point, his interviewer says, "The Son of God who takes away the sins of the world? I wish I could believe in that." And Bono replies,

> "But I love the idea of the Sacrificial Lamb. The point of the death of Christ is that Christ took on the sins of the world, so that our sinful nature does not reap the obvious death. That's

the point ... It's not our own good works that get us through the gates of heaven."[36]

After the history-making meeting in Acts 15, the main battle for the rest of the New Testament (and the rest of Christian history) is to stay on message about grace, and not get distracted by the endless controversies, legalisms, and politics that swoop in like buzzing bugs at a summer picnic to divert our attention from the gospel banquet.

That day, in that meeting, the door was flung open.

"We believe it is through the grace of our Lord Jesus that we are saved, just as they are."

The sign on our house says, "Welcome."

It's hard to keep that sign up, isn't it?

We hang it with the best of intentions. Then *those people* come around, and we discretely take it down and pretend we're not home until they're gone again. You and I replay the scene of the Jerusalem council in our heads throughout our lives. "How could *they* be Christians?"

In our polarized culture, there's an increased push to determine who's in and who's out, to find a litmus test that easily distinguishes real Christians from the false. The problem is, rarely are those tests based on the gospel. We get focused on non-essentials as we try to find cultural or political signifiers that someone is a True Believer.

Later, even Peter lapses back into this, and has to be corrected by the Apostle Paul.

Peter is visiting a local church in Antioch (now part of Turkey) and starts to fear the opinion of the legalistic loud-mouths. So he won't even eat with the very Gentile believers he once publicly defended! Yes! The very man who argued that all food is now kosher and all people are now kosher goes back on both of his revolutionary principles. Paul calls him on it. "I told him face to face that he was wrong!" says Paul. (Galatians 2:11)

And this totally tracks with what we know about up-and-down Peter, doesn't it?

Standing. Then sinking.
Courage. Then cowardice.
Faith. Then fear.

He's one of us for sure! I know I can get excited that God accepts me by grace alone, not by works. But slowly, insidiously, I always seem to slip back into a performance-oriented religion. I judge people. I get cynical.

Keep the welcome sign up. Keep the door open.

Do new believers need to change things about their lives? Of course. Don't you? So let Jesus change them as they walk, stumble, learn, grow, fail, and lead—just like Jesus changed Peter.

I draw three practical applications from Peter's meeting with Cornelius. These may be the most challenging but important habits for Christians in this cultural moment.

1. Stay welcoming.
Jesus came for the outsiders, the outcast, the "other."

2. Stay on message.
Don't get sidetracked by all the polarizing ways both religious and non-religious people are trying to build walls these days. They will try to shame you into "taking a stand" on

issues that can serve no purpose but division. Center yourself on the gospel.

3. Stay ready.

Peter was not up on the roof in Joppa praying about how to reach the Gentiles. He was dreaming of lunch. Then there was a knock on the door.

Listen for that knock. The most unlikely people will suddenly ask you questions. They will share their need. They will ask you to be with them, to spend time talking.

It won't be convenient. Think it was convenient for Peter to travel to Caesarea?

It will be awkward. It was super awkward for Peter.

But it will happen. You will be tired and hungry and sleepy then *knock, knock, knock.* Be ready to answer.

The Holy Spirit is at work, right now, in the most unlikely person. One day the Spirit will put the two of you together. Like Peter and Cornelius.

The Roman architecture in Caesarea Maritime foreshadowed how Peter would spend the end of his life. He would teach—and die—in the heart of the Empire itself.

Peter wrote a letter to early Christians, the book of First Peter in the Bible, that ends with him greeting his readers from what he calls "Babylon." That was a code word used by early Christians for Rome. Over a dozen early Christian writers indicate that Peter died there.

So I decided to end my travels in the spot where Peter ended his.

WHEN SURPRISING DOORS OPEN

Watch a short video for this chapter filmed on location

DIGGING DEEPER
WHAT DID PETER LOOK LIKE?

While the Bible does not contain a physical description of Peter, an ancient portrait was discovered in 2010, in catacombs under an eight-story modern office building in Rome.

This is the earliest known portrait of Peter, dating to the 300s, shortly after the legalization of Christianity. It decorates the tomb of a Roman noblewoman in the Santa Tecla catacomb, which also includes the earliest known images of the apostles John and Andrew. They all came to light thanks to an innovative use of lasers that allowed researchers to delicately burn off centuries of deposits without damaging the original paintings underneath.

It is nearly identical to another ancient portrait of Peter at St. Catherine's Monastery on Mt. Sinai in Egypt. The portraits reveal how consistently early Christians pictured these apostles, and may reflect oral traditions about their appearance. Peter has grey hair and a short grey beard, just like a normal pastor in Santa Cruz.

Icon of Saint Peter from St. Catherine's Monastery on Mt. Sinai (Photo: Wikimedia Commons. This work is in the public domain due to its age)

EPILOGUE

EPILOGUE

ROME
OCTOBER 1962

Dr. Correnti has finally finished his report indicating that the bones in the pope's apartment are not Peter's. He has worked on the case for years and is relieved to finally move on.

But first, Dr. Guarducci has a favor to ask.

The foreman of the Vatican work crews has taken her to a storage room in the basement and led her to a box with bones taken out of the red wall two decades earlier. Would he mind taking a look?

Dr. Correnti opens the box and removes the bones one at a time. He realizes instantly that these are from a single person.

Much later, after extensive analysis, he concludes these are the bones of a man with a robust build, aged sixty to seventy at the time of death. Dr. Correnti identifies bones from nearly every part of the man's body—except the feet, from the ankles down, which are missing entirely. This would match perfectly with the early traditions that Peter had been crucified upside down. It is easy to picture that, in haste to remove the dead body, his legs had been cut off at the ankles, leaving his feet nailed to the cross.

Correnti also notes that at some point, the bones had been wrapped in purple cloth woven with gold threads dating to the late Roman Empire. Intriguingly, the remains in Paul's tomb elsewhere in Rome had also once been wrapped in similar purple cloth with gold filaments. This matches another tradition that in AD 258, during intense persecution under Emperor Valerian, Christians removed the remains of both Peter and Paul from their shrines and hid them in catacombs outside the city. When the persecution *subsided, the remains were restored to their respective tombs wrapped in fine cloth.*

Guarducci compiles a report detailing her work, Correnti's forensic conclusions, and the rest of the archaeological evidence. The report is submitted to five nonreligious scholars for review: Three respected archaeologists and two experts in ancient inscriptions. All five independently agree with her conclusions from the evidence.

Peter's bones have been found.

On December 5, 2013, Pope Francis returns the bones to the niche in the wall where they had rested for over 1800 years, this time not in a marble enclosure but in a Plexiglas box. Peter's bones can now be seen by visitors who ask permission far in advance.

But only a few. Requests must be approved by the Scavi, the Vatican excavation office. Just 15 people are allowed in at a time, accompanied by a trained scholar.

EPILOGUE

I've had the privilege of being one of those fifteen, descending into the earth beneath the basilica to see Peter's bones for myself.

The lighting is dim to preserve the ancient frescoes in the Roman tombs. The air is humid from the water-soaked soil that was once a swamp until the Caesars drained it. The underground street is still paved and lined with elaborate tombs that once stood above ground like little houses.

It's almost a letdown to turn the corner and see the modest shrine built around AD 160 to the memory of Simon Peter.

There is a partial red wall about five feet tall. One white column about a meter high still stands in front of the wall. Along with the other column, now broken, it once supported a small shelf for flowers and other gifts. Predating any of the surrounding Roman tombs, this was just a small memorial on the side of the road for a beloved friend who died nearby, much like the crosses and flowers you might see today on streets where someone was tragically killed.

As I see Simon Peter's simple shrine after so many months of work on this project, I am overcome with emotion. My journey is ending where his earthly journey ended too.

I shift to my left so I can see, within the crumbled walls, the exact spot where Peter's bones were found. And there they are. His earthly remains now rest in a plexiglass box lodged back into the wall where they were first placed by Christians still under Roman threat. It's hard to take in. I am seeing the bones of the man who walked on water with Jesus. Who screamed that he didn't know him. Who opened the door of the church to the world.

The bones are cracked and yellowed with age. For nearly 2,000 years they slept here in the dark, unseen and unknown.

I can't help but contrast this tiny shrine with the massive church 120 feet above my head. I love St. Peter's; its beauty, art, and history are inspiring. Who cannot love Bernini and Michelangelo? But to me, it also symbolizes the halo we've put around Peter's reputation. He was not a soaring, stunning, golden child, somehow gifted from youth to be a saintly leader.

He was just a guy. An inconsistent, impetuous, daring, enthusiastic, doubting, denying, courageous guy, depending on what day you met him. Don't let 20 centuries of well-deserved respect obscure what Peter represents: Jesus calls and loves and forgives and works through flawed followers—and through them, changes the world.

Now I finally see the point of Peter. *This is what a committed Christian looks like.* Not a perfect stained-glass saint. Just a human. Transformed by Christ.

As I stand in front of his tomb, I recall Peter's bold proclamations. At stages in my life, I've said similar words.

Lord, go away from me, I am a sinful man.
Jesus, if it's really you, tell me to come to you.
Lord, save me! I'm drowning!
I believe you are the Christ, the Son of God.
To whom shall I go?
I will never deny you (and two minutes later) *I do not know the man.*
Lord, you know everything. You know that I love you.
Now I see. Now I understand.

Peter has a sentence for every season.

EPILOGUE

I think back to my first big lightbulb moment on this journey. Remember what those early church leaders all said about how Mark wrote his gospel? It was based on material Peter shared in his own sermons.

Then Matthew and Luke borrowed from Mark. That means almost everything we've learned about Peter, we know because Peter told us.

In doing this, what did Peter model?

1. Be authentic about your own walk with Jesus.
Stay transparent about your flaws and failures. Don't just lecture. Tell stories on yourself. The times you got it right. The times you got it wrong. The times you saw Jesus in the storm. The times you were sunk without Jesus. If Peter shared this honestly, and he was a leader of the early church, you can too.

2. Be supportive and patient with those who fail.
When others are honest about their failures, don't condemn them. Encourage that honesty. If you freak out when someone tells you about the time they denied Christ, or about any struggle, you are behaviorally conditioning them to never be that honest with you again. This is why Peter shared these things about himself. To model an atmosphere of honesty for others.

I once saw a church sign: "Nobody is perfect. Anything is possible. Everyone is welcome." Peter's story models this.

3. Point people to Jesus.
Peter's story is not about how he overcame the odds. It's about

Jesus. Peter's not the hero. Jesus is. If lead turns to gold, it's the alchemist we praise, not the lead. Encourage people to come to Jesus in all their complexity and watch him work.

Jesus is not looking for people who think they're fixed. He's looking for people who know they're broken. He calls them and anoints them and transforms them. As Peter writes near the end of his life to all the Christians,

> You also, like living stones, are being built into a spiritual house ... You are a chosen people, a royal priesthood, a holy nation, God's special possession, that you may declare the praises of him who called you out of darkness into his wonderful light. (1 Peter 2:5,9)

Peter was the rock. You also are like living stones.
Peter was chosen. You also are chosen.
Peter was given a mission. You also have been given a mission.

I walk up out of the dark crypt, through the basilica, into sunlit St. Peter's Square.

Towering above the cobblestoned plaza is an ancient Egyptian obelisk that once watched over Nero's Circus. The racetrack, palace, and grandstands have all vanished. Only the obelisk, which stood in the middle of the track, remains. It was likely one of the last things Peter saw before he gazed again at the face of Jesus in heaven.

That obelisk has seen a lot of change.

Today Nero is loathed and Peter is loved.

EPILOGUE

Today people name their dogs Nero and their babies Peter.

Today Nero's palaces have crumbled while Peter's church stands gleaming.

I think of how Simon began his journey, cold and wet and stinking of fish early one morning on the shore of Galilee, where I fished with Razi months before. Now I look around at where he ended up—the center of the world. Peter could never have imagined this when he left his nets.

When you accept Jesus' invitation, you never know where he will lead you.

For Peter? From a fishing boat to the center of the Empire. For you? Only God knows.

But Peter's story shows you this: No matter where the road leads you, and no matter how you stumble, wander, and fall along the way, Jesus never gives up on you. Jesus never stops loving you. Jesus never stops calling you.

So hear him when frightening storms rage around you.

Hear him when his teachings confuse you.

Hear him when you fail miserably.

Hear him when surprising doors swing suddenly open.

Hear him above the dictator's threats.

Hear him even when facing death.

He's saying the same thing each time.

"Follow me."

SMALL GROUP DISCUSSION QUESTIONS

We filmed short videos on the actual locations of each story in this book, which you can find for free at **flawedfollower.com**. I hope that, combined with this book and your Bible reading, the videos will help evoke spiritually productive discussions!

Each week's discussion, including the video, is designed to last about an hour.

CHAPTER 1 DISCUSSION QUESTIONS

TOUCH BASE – 10 MINUTES

Here are some words and phrases that describe Simon Peter. Are there any that could describe you?

Flawed	Impulsive
Underqualified	Brash
Insecure	Stressed
Inadequate	Pressured
Inconsistent	Theologically uneducated
Impetuous	A little arrogant

TAKE IT IN – 10 MINUTES

Read Luke 5:1-11.

Watch the video for "Flawed Follower Week 1" at flawedfollower.com

SMALL GROUP DISCUSSION QUESTIONS

VIDEO NOTES:

TALK IT OUT – 25 TO 35 MINUTES

1. Do you sometimes feel unqualified or inconsistent as a follower of Jesus? In what ways?
   ___ I am drawn to Jesus but don't always get Jesus.
   ___ I am attracted to Jesus, but sometimes wonder if Jesus is attracted to me.
   ___ I vowed never to do that thing again and then did it.
   ___ I sometimes if I should just quit the Jesus thing because I can't live up to it.
   ___ I can be moved by Scripture or transported in worship—and then almost instantly afterward indulge a terrible thought or deed.
   ___ Other:
2. Why do you think it's significant that Jesus calls someone like Simon Peter to be one of his first disciples? How can that encourage you?
3. How does Jesus' simple call to "follow" help clarify what it means to be a Christian?
4. At what point did you begin to understand your Christian faith as a personal choice to follow Jesus—in other words, is there a specific moment or period in your life you can

describe when you realized Jesus was saying, "Follow me"? What did that look like for you?
5. What do you think Jesus meant by being a "fisher of people"? Why do you think Jesus did not just say, "Come and learn a bunch of stuff"?

TAKE IT HOME – 10 MINUTES

How is the Spirit leading you today to be a "fisher of people"? Is there a specific person you are hoping to introduce to Jesus? Or is there someone you feel called to help in some way?

Share what you hope to get from this study of Simon Peter's story.

CLOSE IN PRAYER

Have each group member share a prayer request.

CHAPTER 2 DISCUSSION QUESTIONS

TOUCH BASE – 10 MINUTES

Choose one of these questions to share:

- What is a high and a low you experienced this past week?
- Have you ever been afraid in a storm? Have you ever driven, sailed, or flown through one? What made it frightening?

TAKE IT IN – 10 MINUTES

Read Matthew 14:22-33.

Watch the video for "Flawed Follower Week 2" at flawedfollower.com

VIDEO NOTES:

TALK IT OUT – 25 TO 35 MINUTES

1. What storms of life frighten you right now?
2. What are three things that tend to take your eyes off Jesus and onto the worries or cares or dramas of this world?
3. How can you keep your eyes fixed on Jesus—and what difference do you think this would make in your life, especially related to the three things you mentioned in the previous question?
4. In what way can Jesus' words "Courage I am, do not be afraid" bring you peace?
5. Is there a situation in your life where you need courage to get out of the boat—to try something new? What is it?

TAKE IT HOME – 10 MINUTES

What practical steps can you take this week to spend more time listening to Jesus' voice and less time listening to your fears?

Begin to discuss a group service project. You could collect funds and food for a food bank, volunteer to paint at a school or church, do an act of service for an older adult, or something else you think of! Serving together is another part of following Jesus.

CLOSE IN PRAYER

Have each group member share a prayer request.

CHAPTER 3 DISCUSSION QUESTIONS

TOUCH BASE – 10 MINUTES

Choose one of these questions to share:

- Share a highlight and a lowlight of the week.
- If you could know the answer to any question, what would it be?

TAKE IT IN – 15 MINUTES

Read John 6:22-69 (This is a long passage, so you may want to divide it into five sections this way: John 6:22-27; John 6:28-38; John 6:39-46; John 6:47-58; John 6:59-69)

Watch the video for "Flawed Follower Week 3" at flawedfollower.com

SMALL GROUP DISCUSSION QUESTIONS

VIDEO NOTES:

TALK IT OUT – 25 TO 35 MINUTES

1. Do you identify with the people challenged by Jesus' words in that synagogue? How?
2. Which of these statements from the gospels do you identify with:
   "This is a hard teaching."
   "Lord, to whom shall we go?"
   "You have the words of eternal life."
   "I believe; help my unbelief."
3. The invitation of Jesus is specifically to "follow me." How is this different than saying "understand me," "sign this doctrinal statement for me," or "have no further questions about me"? How is "follow me" different from what many people perceive it means to be a Christian?
4. Have you ever come to a crisis of faith, when you wondered whether to continue or abandon it? Have you resolved it? If so, how?
5. Read John 6:66-68. How might Peter's conversation with Jesus help your walk of faith, even through your doubts and trials?
6. Apparently, some in that crowd were following Jesus when they got something fun out of it: Free wine, free dinner,

free healing ... but when he challenged some of their ideas, they were gone.

Similarly, sociologist Christian Smith coined the phrase "Moralistic Therapeutic Deism" (MTD) to describe the actual religious beliefs of many Americans. They may use the term "Christian," but in actuality, they see salvation as coming by good behavior; they see the purpose of Jesus as increasing their sense of well-being; and they see God vaguely as "the man upstairs." Did you ever have a more vague view of Jesus like that? When did your view of Jesus come into sharper focus? What happened?

TAKE IT HOME – 10 MINUTES

Jesus is always compassionate, humble, and gentle. Yet he is not usually interested in making himself absolutely easy to understand or pleasing people. He leaves a lot of puzzling statements hanging in midair, as he does in John 6. Why do you think this is? What can this teach you about following Jesus?

Have you decided on a group service project? Choose your project, decide on a date, and choose project coordinators.

CLOSE IN PRAYER

Have each group member share a prayer request.

CHAPTER 4 DISCUSSION QUESTIONS

TOUCH BASE – 10 MINUTES

Choose one of these questions to share:

- What is a high and a low you experienced this past week?
- Name something that makes you happy

TAKE IT IN – 10 MINUTES

Watch the video for "Flawed Follower Week 4" at flawedfollower.com

VIDEO NOTES:

TALK IT OUT – 25 TO 35 MINUTES

1. Read Matthew 16:13-20. Jesus asks, "Who do you say I am?" Why is this question so important—why this instead of, "What do you think of my teaching?"
2. What had Jesus done to this point that may have moved Peter to conclude that Jesus was the Messiah?
3. Jesus wants these disciples to make a personal conclusion: "Who do you say I am?" Have you arrived at a moment when you made your faith personal? When and how did that happen for you?
4. Read Matthew 16:21-23. How do Peter's two responses show that he is both accurate and inaccurate about Jesus?
5. What does the fact that Peter is both a rock and stumbling block within five verses teach you about Christian growth? How could you apply this in your setting (to your children, your friends, your fellow Christians)?
6. Why do you think the gospel writers chose to describe Peter's leadership role—and yet they also keep highlighting his misunderstandings, mistakes, breakdowns, and failures? How do you respond to seeing both sides of Peter?
7. Read Matthew 16:24-27. The way of Jesus is suffering and service. That is our calling, too.

SMALL GROUP DISCUSSION QUESTIONS

Read these verses:

For God called you to do good, even if it means suffering, just as Christ suffered for you. He is your example, and you must follow in his steps. (1 Peter 2:21 NLT)

You must have the same attitude that Christ Jesus had. Though he was God, he did not think of equality with God as something to cling to. Instead, he gave up his divine privileges; he took the humble position of a slave and was born as a human being. When he appeared in human form, he humbled himself in obedience to God and died a criminal's death on a cross. (Philippians 2:5-8 NLT)

(Jesus said after washing his disciples' feet) "You call me 'Teacher' and 'Lord,' and rightly so, for that is what I am. Now that I, your Lord and Teacher, have washed your feet, you also should wash one another's feet. I have set you an example that you should do as I have done for you." (John 13:13-15)

Is it possible for Christians today, like Peter in today's story, to sincerely get the *identity* of Jesus as Messiah and Son of God—yet totally miss the *way* of Jesus as suffering servants? How do you see this happening?

TAKE IT HOME – 10 MINUTES

What is one practical way this week that you can represent not just the *who* of Jesus, but also the *way* of Jesus, through service and sacrifice?

CLOSE IN PRAYER

Have each group member share a prayer request.

CHAPTER 5 DISCUSSION QUESTIONS

TOUCH BASE – 10 MINUTES

Choose one of these questions to share:

- What is a high and a low you experienced this past week?
- Who do you relate to more: someone who is heroic, strong, and seemingly flawless, or someone flawed and transparent about their weaknesses? Why?

TAKE IT IN – 10 MINUTES

Watch the video for "Flawed Follower Week 5" at flawedfollower.com

VIDEO NOTES:

1. Why do you think all four gospels include this story of Peter's failure—even though he was a well-loved figure among the early Christians? Is there any comfort you gain from Peter's story of failure? How can failure or relapse be part of growth?
2. Read Mark 14:27-31. Peter insists that even if all the other disciples fell away, he would never fall. Humorously, the other disciples insist the same thing is true of them! Why do you think most people tend to rate themselves "better" in comparison to others? Why is this a danger?
3. Read Mark 14:66-72. Which of the three common reasons for failure do you most identify with?
   __ I overestimate my strength
   __ I fear disapproval
   __ I speak from insecurity and exhaustion
4. In chapter 5, Rene mentions three means of recovery from a fall. How have you seen God use these in your own life?
   __ Grief
   __ Groups
   __ Grace
5. Read Luke 22:31-32. Which of these three statements is most difficult for you to believe in practice?
   __ Jesus is never shocked when you fall.

__ Jesus welcomes you back when you fall.

__ Jesus prays for you when you fall.

6. How might you be tempted to "deny Christ" in the world today?
7. Was there ever a moment in your life when you heard the rooster crow, so to speak, and suddenly realized with clarity that you had crossed a line or had a character flaw and needed to change? What happened?

TAKE IT HOME – 10 MINUTES

In your own life, have you learned a practical lesson or helpful tip about resisting temptation that you can share with the group?

What guardrails can you put back up in your life this week to keep from falling?

CLOSE IN PRAYER

Have each group member share a prayer request.

CHAPTER 6 DISCUSSION QUESTIONS

TOUCH BASE – 10 MINUTES

1. Choose one of these questions to share:

   - What is a high and a low you experienced this past week?
   - Is there a certain smell that triggers emotions or memories for you?
   - What are some of your best memories of camping? What are the *smells* of camping for you?

TAKE IT IN – 10 MINUTES

Watch the video for "Flawed Follower Week 6" at flawedfollower.com

SMALL GROUP DISCUSSION QUESTIONS

VIDEO NOTES:

TALK IT OUT – 25 TO 35 MINUTES

1. What are some of the emotions Peter might have experienced as he saw and smelled the charcoal fire Jesus prepared?
2. How do you sometimes struggle with a pervading sense of guilt?
3. Based on this story in John 21, how does Jesus respond when you fail?
4. Read these passages and describe what they say about God's forgiveness:
   Romans 3:23-24
   Romans 8:1
   Ephesians 1:7-8
   Psalm 103:11-12
5. In John 21, what is the connection between "Do you love me?" and "Then tend my lambs?" How does our care for others show our love for Jesus?

TAKE IT HOME – 10 MINUTES

Who is a "lamb" of Jesus you can care for this week or as part of your group's project?

If you have done your group service project, you have "served his lambs." How is an act of service to others also an act of love toward Jesus?

CLOSE IN PRAYER

Have each group member share a prayer request.

SMALL GROUP DISCUSSION QUESTIONS

CHAPTER 7 DISCUSSION QUESTIONS

TOUCH BASE – 10 MINUTES

Have each group member share a highlight and a lowlight from the week.

If you could live in a different country for a year, which country would you choose?

TAKE IT IN – 15 MINUTES

Read Acts 10:21-48. (This is a longish passage, so you may want to divide it among three people like this: Acts 10:21-33; Acts 10:34-43; Acts 10:44-48)
Watch the video for "Flawed Follower Week 7" at flawedfollower.com

VIDEO NOTES:

TALK IT OUT – 25 TO 35 MINUTES

1. Read Acts 15:11. How are we saved, according to Peter?

Grace means God lavishes his blessings on us, including salvation from sin, without cost. We do not earn it. We receive it. Understanding biblical grace can change everything about how you perceive your religion, your motivations, God, others ... in fact, life itself!

The following chart may help you see how this happens. Which side of this chart are you on?

SMALL GROUP DISCUSSION QUESTIONS

PERFORMANCE-ORIENTED RELIGION	THE GOSPEL OF GRACE
"I obey, therefore I'm accepted"	"I'm accepted, therefore I obey"
Motivation: Fear and insecurity	Motivation: Security and grateful joy
Identity: Based on my performance; therefore criticism is devastating	Identity: Based on God's love for me therefore criticism may be a struggle but is taken much less personally
My prayer life is largely obligation; I feel I must pray more, and pray better.	My prayer life is relaxed and has stretches of praise and adoration
Self-image: Swings between two extremes: I can feel proud and impatient with "lesser performers" when I am doing well, then when I fall, I feel like a miserable failure.	Self-image: I see myself as both sinful and yet also fully loved by God, lavished with his grace though I am undeserving.
My self-worth is based mainly on how hard I work or how moral I am—and I find myself looking down on the "lazy" or "immoral."	My self-image is centered on the One who died for me. I am saved by sheer grace so how could I look down on anyone?

(Chart adapted from *Gospel in Life: Grace Changes Everything* by Tim Keller)

2. The Bible verse most frequently quoted by the Bible itself—it is repeated, paraphrased, and referenced at least 20 times—is about God's grace: "The LORD is merciful and gracious, slow to anger and filled with unfailing love and faithfulness." (Exodus 34:6) How is this different from the way many people see God?
How would it impact your life if you genuinely believed that verse every day to the core of your being?
3. Why is it easy to relapse into a works-oriented view of religion rather than grace? Has this ever happened to you? If so, what brought you back to grace?
4. If "keeping rules" is not the correct biblical gauge for measuring spiritual health, then what is? (See Galatians 5:22-23)
5. When Peter accepted Jesus' invitation to "follow me," he had no idea of the places he would go or the amazing things he would do. Everything about his life changed, from his worldview to his home. Has following Jesus led to any surprising changes or growth in your life?

TAKE IT HOME – 10 MINUTES

What does Peter's life's transformation tell you about the forgiveness of Jesus and the power of the Holy Spirit?

As we wrap up our look at Peter's life, what life lesson will you take away from this study?

CLOSE IN PRAYER

Have each group member share a prayer request.

ACKNOWLEDGEMENTS

My deepest thanks to my wife Laurie who traveled with me in Simon Peter's path, organized all the travel, and encouraged me along every step of the journey. She was also an invaluable reader of early versions of the book, along with Jonathan Schlaepfer, Don Miller, Brian Bonn, Valerie Webb, and Jim Josselyn. They all caught innumerable mistakes and made vast improvements. Any remaining errors are all my fault and not theirs. I was delighted to partner with Julie, Ryan and Molly at Mayfly Design, who creatively crafted the cover and interior of this book. The talented Jamie Rom and her husband Steve were our two-person film crew in Israel. I always marvel at how Jamie takes our tiny budgets and makes the videos look like a million bucks. After Jamie and Steve welcomed baby Oliver into the world, David Schlaepfer expertly did the final edits, graphics, and production. Thanks also to Jared Booye for designing the web site for flawedfollower.com in record time. I can't imagine the difficulty Jessica Pizarro had in translating my quirky words into Spanish, but she did it, and I am so grateful. I am beyond honored to have had the prestigious Richie Biggs record, edit, and mix the audiobook. He did this purely as a ministry, yet applied all his formidable professional skill to the end product. Thank you Richie! Finally, I am beyond grateful to Valerie Webb for shepherding this project from inception to completion. What a team! Thank you Lord for all the help you provided to this very flawed follower.

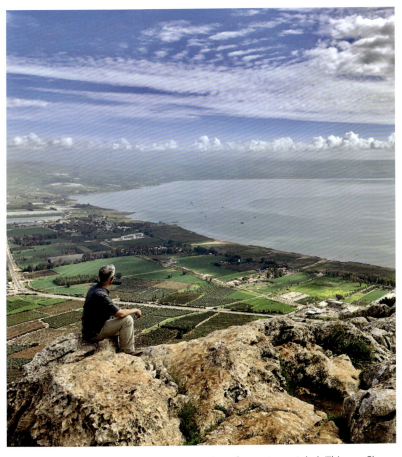

Looking out over the Sea of Galilee's north shore from Mount Arbel. This was Simon Peter's neighborhood, encompassing Capernaum, Bethsaida, and Magdala

Fishing with Razi and his crew on the Sea of Galilee

Razi heading out expectantly for a morning of fishing.

We fished patiently and caught... one sardine.

While out on the Sea of Galilee one day a storm suddenly blew in. This is the moment we saw it coming. White caps kicked up, clouds grew dark, the wind howled, and soon the shore was invisible.

This is the moment the storm ended, with rays of sunshine promising calm waters

The author paddleboarding on the Sea of Galilee (and pretending to walk on water)
Photo credit: Hod Froilch

Rembrandt's only seascape, *Christ in the Storm on the Sea of Galilee*, the rarest object stolen in the art heist at Boston's Gardner Museum (Public Domain)

The synagogue in Capernaum from the era of Jesus and Peter stood here. The ruins are mostly from a later remodel, but the original black basalt foundations are still visible. This is where Jesus preached the sermon in John 6.

The author stands at the Cave of Pan in the massive cliff at Caesarea Philippi. This is the area where Jesus said to Peter, "Upon this rock I will build my church."

View of Jerusalem from the Mount of Olives, where Jesus was arrested.

At dawn on the Sea of Galilee after a night of net fishing

The ancient port of Joppa, or Jaffa, as it is known today, where Peter saw the vision in Acts 10.

This massive seaside chariot racetrack is just one of the astonishing ruins from the Roman colony of Caesarea Maritime, where Peter met Cornelius.

St. Peter's Basilica in Rome, built over the ancient memorial to Peter's martyrdom

The obelisk In St. Peter's Square in Rome is the only surviving element from Nero's Circus, where Peter was probably martyred.

The author outside the office of the Vatican Excavations, about to descend underground to see the bones of Peter himself. Photos of the tomb are not permitted.

ENDNOTES

PROLOGUE:

1. Although these details of Peter's death are not in the New Testament, many early Christian writers passed them along, including the First Epistle of Clement, which was written by Clement, the bishop of Rome, to the church in Corinth around AD 95. It is the earliest known document alluding to Peter's martyrdom in Rome (I Clement 5:4). Tertullian, writing around AD 200, specifically states that Peter was crucified in Rome by Nero, as quoted by Elwell and Yarbrough, *Encountering the New Testament* (Grand Rapids: Baker Press, 1998), 88. Soon afterward, Origen specifies that Peter was crucified upside-down at his own request (as quoted by Eusebius of Caesarea, *Ecclesiastical History*, 3.1.2)
2. Thomas J. Craughwell, *St. Peter's Bones* (New York: Image, 2013), 12.
3. Ibid.

CHAPTER 1

4. Papias, who was born in AD 60, wrote that "Mark, having become the interpreter of Peter, wrote down accurately whatsoever he remembered." Irenaeus, born in AD 115, said, "Mark, the disciple and interpreter of Peter, did also hand down to us in writing what had been preached by Peter." https://drjimsebt.com/2023/04/24/2-church-fathers-and-marks-gospel/
5. Athenaeus, *The Deipnosophists*, Book VI (C. D. Yonge, B.A., Ed.) https://www.perseus.tufts.edu/hopper/text?doc=Perseus:abo:tlg,0008,001:6 accessed May 6, 2024.
6. You can also see international influence in the names of the disciples. His parents named Peter "Simon," or in Hebrew "Shimon." Five other disciples also have Hebrew names. But some have purely Greek names. Philip was apparently named for Alexander the Great's famous father. Thaddaeus is also a Greek name. These names reflect the primary cultural tension of the time: Jew vs. Gentile.
7. Carmine Gallo, "How Steve Jobs And Bill Gates Inspired John Sculley To Pursue The 'Noble Cause'" Forbes, Nov 12, 2016 https://www.forbes.com/sites/carminegallo/2016/11/12/how-steve-jobs-and-bill-gates-inspired-john-sculley-to-pursue-the-noble-cause/?sh=217aec04232b accessed Feb 22, 2024.
8. Brennan Manning, *The Ragamuffin Gospel: Good News for the Bedraggled, Beat-Up, and Burnt Out*, (Portland: Multnomah, 2005) p. 29.
9. Arthur Brooks, "How to Find Your Faith," *The Atlantic*, April 25, 2024 Accessed May 1, 2024.
10 Aaron Damiani, "Useful Spiritual Practices," *Christianity Today* July/August 2024 p 121)
11. Manning, p. 68.

CHAPTER 2

12. I have greatly simplified the fascinating and labyrinthine tale of the Vatican excavations—without, I hope, getting the general narrative wrong. Readers looking for book-length treatment of the archaeological digs, and the soap-opera scandals and intrigue that accompanied them, are directed to Thomas J. Craughwell, *St. Peter's Bones* (New York: Image, 2013), John O'Neill, *The Fisherman's Tomb* (Huntington, IN: Our Sunday Visitor, 2028), and John Evangelist Walsh, *The Bones of St. Peter* (New York: Doubleday, 1982), the text of the latter also available for free online at https://stpetersbasilica.info/Necropolis/JW/TheBonesofStPeter-8.htm
13. Some people point to the supposed spirit of Samuel who is called up in a séance at the behest of King Saul in 1 Samuel 28:5-20 as an exception. I do not believe this was actually Samuel's ghost. I think this story is meant to show Saul's state of mind—his utter terror and gullibility. Look at the passage closely. First, Samuel never actually appears. The woman holding the séance says "an old man wearing a robe is coming up." Saul just assumes from this sparse description, which surely matched a thousand men, that the spirit was Samuel. Second, the prophecy given by "Samuel" is false. He says that Israel will be conquered by the Philistines, and that Saul and all his sons would die. This did not happen. Saul took his own life. At least one of his sons survived: Ish-bosheth, who later fought David for the crown. Israel was not conquered by the Philistines. The biblical standard for ascertaining whether someone is a true prophet is 100% accuracy (Deuteronomy 18:20-22). The Bible's own standard proves this was not Samuel.
14. Jesus probably spoke these words in Aramaic, a local dialect derived from Hebrew, but the gospels were written in Greek, which was understood worldwide at the time. So Greek is the closest we can get to Jesus' actual words. Although it needs to be said that then, like today in practically the entire world except the USA, it was very common for people to speak multiple languages. The gospels show Jesus reading Hebrew, speaking both Hebrew and Aramaic with his disciples, and speaking with Roman centurions and administrators who probably did not know either of those languages. It's likely that he spoke Greek with them. Some of the inscriptions on ossuaries (boxes for the bones of deceased relatives) found from first-century Israel are written in Greek. These are graves not of Romans but of devout Jewish residents of Jerusalem, demonstrating the prevalence of Greek even among Jews of the time. So it is possible that at times Jesus also spoke Greek to other Jews. For more on this topic, see G. Scott Gleaves, "Did Jesus Speak Greek?" *Ancient Near East Today* (October 2015, Vol. 3, No. 10)
15. John Ortberg, *If You Want to Walk on Water, You've Got to Get Out of the Boat* (Grand Rapids: Zondervan, 2001), 33.

CHAPTER 3

16. https://stpetersbasilica.info/Necropolis/JW/TheBonesofStPeter-6.htm accessed April 10, 2024.
17. Christian Smith with Denton Lundquist, *Soul Searching: The Religious and Spiritual Lives of American Teenagers* (New York: Oxford University Press, 2005) 165.
18. Tim Keller, https://quarterly.gospelinlife.com/reconstructing-faith/ accessed March 27, 2024.

CHAPTER 4

19. Craughwell, 85.
20. In John's Gospel, Jesus gives Simon the new name "Peter" on the day he's called to be a disciple. John often organizes his gospel by theme rather than by a strict chronology. For example, John places the Temple cleansing at the beginning of Jesus' ministry rather than at the end as the four synoptic gospels do. This is not a mistake. John wrote his account

ENDNOTES

last, so he knows what the other gospels recorded very well. John likes to play with time, foreshadowing the tension to come, like a Christopher Nolan movie.
21. Marc Chalufour (February 23, 2023). "What's Behind Boom of Christianity in China?" *The Brink: Pioneering Research from Boston University*. Accessed on 19 October, 2023 at https://www.bu.edu/articles/2023/why-is-christianity-growing-in-china/
22. For example, Ahishar was Solomon's deputy (1 Kings 4:6), and Arza was King Elah's deputy (1 Kings 16:9).
23. Rula Mansour, "When the Cannons are Rumbling, the Sermon on the Mount Doesn't Remain Silent," https://www.comeandsee.com/view.php?sid=1426 accessed May 4, 2024.

CHAPTER 5

24. Pliny, Letters 10.96-97
25. https://www.haaretz.com/archaeology/2016-07-12/ty-article/priestly-quarter-of-ancient-jerusalem-found-on-mt-zion/0000017f-db87-d856-a37f-ffc76c7f0000
26. Pesachim 57a, 284-285.
27. Josephus - *Antiquities of the Jews* 20.9.2-4.
28. Adam Hamilton, *Simon Peter*, Nashville: Abingdon Press, 2028, 105.

CHAPTER 6

29. Craughwell, 117.
30. Vance Havner, *Hearts Afire: Light on Successful Soul Winning* (Westwood, NJ: Fleming H. Revell, 1952), 76.
31. Rick Warren, *The Purpose Driven Life*, (Grand Rapids: Zondervan, 2012) 251, 265.
32. Ray Johnston, *Hope Quotient*, (Nashville, Tennessee: W Publishing, an imprint of Thomas Nelson, 2014) 211-214.
33. Craughwell, 127.

CHAPTER 7

34. N.T. Wright, *Acts for Everyone, Vol. 1*, (Louisville, Kentucky: Westminster John Knox Press, 2008), 177.
35. Josephus, W 2.17.2 408-410.
36. Michka Assayas, *Bono: In Conversation with Michka Assayas* (New York: Riverhead, 2005).